LEARN TO BE YOUR OWN LAWYER
IN 30 DAYS

A Complete Guide For Everybody

ANKOOSH MEHTA

JAICO PUBLISHING HOUSE
Ahmedabad Bangalore Bhopal Chennai
Delhi Hyderabad Kolkata Lucknow Mumbai

Published by Jaico Publishing House
A-2 Jash Chambers, 7-A Sir Phirozshah Mehta Road
Fort, Mumbai - 400 001
jaicopub@jaicobooks.com
www.jaicobooks.com

© Ankoosh Mehta

LEARN TO BE YOUR OWN LAWYER IN 30 DAYS
ISBN 978-81-7992-825-7

First Jaico Impression: 2008
Third Jaico Impression: 2010

No part of this book may be reproduced or utilized in
any form or by any means, electronic or
mechanical including photocopying, recording or by any
information storage and retrieval system,
without permission in writing from the publishers.

Printed by
Pashupati Printers (P) Ltd., Delhi-95

Disclaimer

This book does not represent or endorse the accuracy of any advice, opinion, statement or other information it contains. It is not covered by any syllabus of any university in or outside India, and it is not meant to be cited as an authority before any court/tribunal or statutory authority.

Neither the author nor the publisher will be responsible for any action taken by a reader on the basis of this book. The sample Agreements, specimens may differ from state to state.

Contents

FOREWORD	viii
PREFACE	ix

PART I - CIVIL MATTERS

1. Consumer Protection	2
2. Partnership	8
3. Competency To Contract	18
4. Indemnity & Guarantee	23
5. Negotiable Instruments	28
6. Trusts	32
7. Power Of Attorney	36
8. Purchase & Sale Of Goods	40
9. Principal & Agent	46

PART II - PROPERTY MATTERS

1. Sale	52
2. Mortgage	61
3. Lease	68
4. Exchange	74
5. Gift	78
6. Lis Pendens	84
7. Charge On Property	86
8. Part Performance	88
9. Transfer Of property to An Unborn Person	91

PART III - CORPORATE MATTERS

1. Types Of Companies	94

2. Incorporation	97
3. Meetings	100
4. Resolutions	102
5. Shares	105
6. Buy-Back Of Shares & Employee Stock Option Scheme	108
7. Directors	110
8. Other Managerial Personnel	113
9. Amalgamation	116
10. Winding Up Of A Company	120

PART IV - CRIMINAL MATTERS

1. Cheque Dishonour	126
2. Property Related Crimes	132
3. Counterfeiting	135
4. Offences Relating to Religion	138
5. Forgery	141
6. Crimes Against Women	144
7. Murder & Culpable Homicide	147
8. Words & Phrases	151
9. First Information Report	154
10. Bail	158
11. Defamation	161
12. Offences Against The Government & Armed Forces	165

PART V - LAW OF TORTS

1. What Is A Tort?	170
2. Nuisance	172
3. Trespass To Goods	175
4. Negligence	178
5. Master & Servant Relation	182
6. Trespass Of Immoveable Property	185
7. Libel, Slander & Innuendo	188
8. Strict & Liability	190

PART VI - CONSTITUTION OF INDIA

1. Citizenship — 196
2. Right To Freedom — 198
3. Right To Equality — 200
4. Fundamental Duties — 203
5. The Parliament (Union Legislature) — 204
6. State Legislature — 207
7. Emergency — 210
8. Elections — 212
9. The President, Vice President, Council of Ministers & Prime Minister — 214
10. Judiciary — 217

PART VII - OTHER IMPORTANT PROVISIONS

1. Marriage & Divorce — 222
2. Will & Probate — 227
3. Duties Of A Lawyer — 231
4. Law Of Limitation — 233
5. Arbitration — 236
6. Right To Information — 242
7. Human Rights — 245
8. Intellectual Property Rights — 247
9. Public Interest Litigations (PIL) — 249
10. Protection of Wild Life — 251
11. Equal Opportunities for Persons With Disabilities — 254
12. Settlement Of disputes — 259
13. Contempt of Court — 260
14. Appeal — 262
15. Suit By Or Against The Government — 264
16. Evidence — 266
17. Film & Television Agreements — 269
18. Legal Terms — 288

S.P. Bharucha
Former Chief Justice of India

2-B " SAMATA",
General Bhosle Marg,
Mumbai - 400 021.

Foreword

Though he may have heard of a contract and may know, broadly, what it connotes, it is very unlikely that a layman would have any notion of what the law on the subject of contracts is. This book seeks to explain in simple terms all the commoner branches of the law, civil and criminal, which the layman is likely to encounter, and the terms specific thereto. Thus, the book explains what a negotiable instrument is and, within that branch of the law, what cheques and hundis are.

As a reference book for the layman, the book is of inestimable value. It should find a place in the libraries of laymen who frequently interact with the law. It should, certainly, be in all public libraries.

The author is a young solicitor. In thinking of this book, he has had a great idea; and he has put in great effort in collating the subjects that it addresses and in explaining them in language that is not difficult to understand. I trust that this publication in English will prove sufficiently popular to encourage him to contemplate translations in the vernacular.

S.P. Bharucha

Place : Mumbai.
Date : 16th November, 2007.

Preface

This book is written for professionals including chartered accountants, doctors and bankers as well as for activists, actors, disabled persons, wild life supporters and above all, for the common man.

The book is segregated into seven parts, each having sub-parts for better understanding of the subject. The book has covered more than 70 topics on law and legal issues and wherever necessary, specimen agreements and contracts have been included.

- Part I deals with topics on civil matters. This includes:
  - Consumer Protection - Extensively covers the meaning of the word Consumer, deals with his rights and his redressal agencies.
  - Partnership - Discussions on the terms Partnership, Goodwill and whether a minor can become a partner. A specimen of a partnership agreement has also been included.
  - Negotiable Instruments - Explains the meaning and relevance of promissory notes, bills of exchange and cheques.
- Part II outlines transactions related to immoveable property. The legalities behind a sale, mortgage, lease or gift etc have been explained.,
  - Also includes the preparation of sale agreements, lease agreements and gift agreements.
  - A separate discussion outlines whether an unborn person is entitled to property.
- Part III is specifically assigned to matters concerning companies and share-

holders. It includes provisions relating to setting up of companies, directors, buy-back of shares, winding up, amalgamation of companies, etc.

- Part IV outlines certain important provisions relating to criminal law, such as cheque bouncing, offences relating to religion, crimes against women and dowry death, murder and suicide, anticipatory bail and defamation.

- Part V carries discussions on the rights of an individual that arise independent of any contract. For example, if the corporation of a certain locality has been carrying out road repairs every night and have dug up some parts of the roads, then it is the duty of the corporation to ensure that precautions such as warning signs and proper lighting are in place, to ensure the safety of motorists and pedestrians.

    A separate chapter, emphasizes the meaning of the word Negligence, and the persons it covers. For example: It is the duty of a chocolate manufacturing company to ensure that its products (chocolates) are fit for human consumption. If the company fails to perform its duty towards its consumers, it is liable.

    How words or signs take the character of Libel, Slander and Innuendo have also been explained.

- Part VI informs the reader about certain relevant aspects of the Constitution of India such as who is a citizen of India., The Right to Freedom and the Right to Equality. The circumstances under which an Emergency can be declared in a state or the country, and the person who has the authority to do so, are discussed. The right to vote and the necessary qualifications have also been explained.

- Part VII deals with a host of different topics relating to marriage and divorce, preparation of a Will, Right to Information Act, protection of wild life, equal opportunities for persons with disabilities, intellectual property rights, film and television contracts etc.

Part I
Civil Matters

1

Consumer Protection

The law governing the consumer is the Consumer Protection Act. We all are consumers in some form or the other. This discussion aims to shed some light on our rights and remedies as consumers.

WHAT IS CONSUMER PROTECTION?

Consumer Protection is protection taken in the interest of the consumer. There are consumer councils and other authorities which have been set up for redressing the grievances of the consumer.

WHO IS A CONSUMER?

A consumer is any person who buys goods for a consideration which, he pays or promises to pay, or partly pays and partly promises to pay. A consumer also includes a *user* of goods bought, other than the person who has paid the consideration for the same. However, a person who buys goods only for the purposes of resale or for commercial purposes is not a consumer.

■ Example : Ajinkya Co. Ltd. purchases large quantities of thread for sewing machines, for the mass production of cloth, which will generate huge profits. Ajinkya Co. Ltd. is not a consumer.

Any person who hires or avails of any *services* for a consideration paid or promised to be paid, and the beneficiary of such a person is also a consumer. Thus, a consumer includes a person who avails of both goods and services.

GOODS AND SERVICE

Goods means and includes every kind of moveable property. Furniture, books, clothes, pens etc. are all goods.

Service means a service of any description which is made available to persons desirous of availing them.

Banking, financing, insurance, supply of electricity, boarding or lodging or both, entertainment, etc are all services.

Rendering of any service free of charge or under a contract of personal service does not constitute a service.

■ Example : Ramesh is a cook for the Shah family. The Shah family is not a consumer in this respect and Ramesh does not render service as stated above.

A user of electricity or telephone connection; a customer in a restaurant; patients in a hospital availing medical treatment; a tourist going on a conducted tour etc. are all consumers.

College students; a devotee in a temple, etc, are not consumers.

COMPLAINT AND COMPLAINANT

When a consumer is dissatisfied with the goods purchased or services availed of by him, he is entitled to file a Complaint.

A complaint is an allegation in writing made by the complainant on either of the following grounds :

(i) the trader or service provider has adopted an *unfair trade practice.*

(ii) the goods bought by the complainant are *defective.*

(iii) the services availed of are *deficient.*

(iv) a trader or service provider has charged a price more than the price fixed by law or displayed on the goods or agreed between the parties.

(v) the goods or services which are being offered for sale or which are being provided are *hazardous* to life and safety.

A Complainant may be a consumer, a registered consumer association, the Central or State Government or the legal heir of a deceased consumer.

UNFAIR TRADE PRACTICE

This means a deceptive practice adopted for the purpose of promoting the sale or use of any goods or services.

■ Example : A vegetarian restaurant, A1 Foods falsely states that it has been awarded the best vegetarian restaurant award, in order to attract more customers, when actually, it was not so.

DEFECT

This refers to any fault or shortcoming in the quality, quantity or standard of goods which is required to be maintained by law or as claimed by the trader.

DEFICIENCY

This refers to any fault or imperfection in the quality, nature or manner of performance, as required by law or undertaken to be performed by any person in relation to any services.

RELEVANT SERVICES

Some relevant services are:

Courier Services

It is the responsibility of a courier service company to ensure that the mail/parcel is delivered safely and on time to the addressee. At the time of delivery, it is obligatory on the part of the courier company to take the receiver's signature/acknowledgement that the mail/parcel has been received.

■ Example : Mr. Jatakia was sending a sample of certain types of paper meant for export to his customer in Sao Paulo, Brazil. The said sample was urgently required. He approached Quick Time Courier Company for delivering the parcel, and was assured that the parcel would reach within 48 hours. After one week, his customer informed him that the parcel had not arrived. On making inquiries with the courier agency, it was revealed that the parcel was lost. Mr. Jatakia successfully filed a claim for loss of business and damages against the courier company.

Advocates

Advocates are bound professionally and ethically, to protect the interest of their clients and to fight for their rights. An advocate cannot make any commitment or waive any right on behalf of his client, unless his client has authorized him to do so. An advocate is not entitled to retain papers of his client if his fees have not been paid. An advocate cannot advise the two parties who are opposing each other at the same time.

■ Example : Workers of Rajendra Fertilizers approached an advocate, Shyamlal to represent them against their employers, for the non-payment of their wages since January, 2004. Shyamlal was explained the finer details of the case and was specifically told that the employers had obtained false receipts from the workers stating that their wages were paid. When the matter came up for hearing Shyamlal did not dispute the receipts produced by the employer's advocate . This resulted in a loss of substantial money to the workers. The workers brought an action against their advocate, which was allowed, and Shyamlal was directed to pay damages to the workers.

Hotels

Hotels are also a part of the service industry. It is their duty to ensure the care, comfort and safety of their customers. The rooms must be in proper condition. For instance, where the electrical appliances are not working, it is the hotel's responsibility to have the same repaired or to provide the customer with a new room, without further inconvenience.

■ Example : Mr. Arjun Saxena had booked himself and his family of four, in Star Hotel, Bangalore from the first to the seventh of March, 2003. The reservations were made and money was paid in advance, in Mumbai. However, on the said date, when Mr. Saxena reached the hotel, he was informed that it was fully booked and that there was no reservation in his name. After seeking the advice of his lawyer, Mr. Saxena preferred an action against the hotel. The hotel was directed to reimburse Mr. Saxena and his family, for the expenses incurred, along with travel costs and damages.

CONSUMER DISPUTES REDRESSAL AGENCIES

a. The District Forum, in each district of the state.

b. The State Commission.

c. The National Commission.

This is the three-tier system for consumer redressal.

DISTRICT FORUM

The District Forum has jurisdiction to entertain complaints where the value of the goods or services (and compensation, if any) claimed, does not exceed Rs. 20 lakhs.

A complaint before the District Forum can be filed where the opposite party or parties are either residing or working within its jurisdiction. When there are more than one opposite parties residing within different districts, the complaint may be filed in the District Forum with its permission or with the consent of the other opposite parties. Lastly, a complaint may also be filed before the Forum within whose jurisdiction the 'cause of action' arose in whole or in part. Cause of action means every fact which is necessary to be proved to entitle the complainant to relief.

■ Example : Ajay Singh, who lives in Mumbai Central, purchases a washing machine of a reputed brand from an authorized agent in Thane. (A district on the outskirts of Mumbai). The head office of the washing machine company is in Flora Fountain, Mumbai. The washing machine stops working on the third day itself. Ajay can file a complaint in the District Forum, either where the washing machine was purchased from (i.e. Thane) or in the Forum within whose jurisdiction the head office of the company is located.

STATE COMMISSION

The State Commission will have jurisdiction to entertain complaints where the value of goods or services (including compensation, if any) claimed exceeds

Rs. 20 lakh but is less than Rs. 1 crore. The Commission has jurisdiction to entertain appeals against the District Forum.

The provisions as regards the State Commission before which a complaint can be filed are similar to that of the District Forum.

NATIONAL COMMISSION

The National Commission has jurisdiction to entertain complaints where the value of goods or services (and compensation, if any) claimed exceed Rupees one crore. It has the power to call for the case pending before a State Commission, if it feels that the State Commission has failed to exercise its jurisdiction or acted in excess of its jurisdiction or has acted illegally or irregularly.

A person aggrieved by an order of the National Commission can prefer an Appeal to the Supreme Court of India.

The District Forum, the State Commission or the National Commission shall not admit any complaint unless it is filed within "two years" from the date on which the cause of action has arisen, unless the complainant gives sufficient reasons for not filing the complaint within such period.

FRIVOLOUS OR VEXATIOUS COMPLAINTS

Where either of the three forums come to a conclusion that the complaint filed is frivolous, or where the complainant has come with unclean hands, an order directing the complainant to pay the opposite party, a maximum of rupees ten thousand and dismissing the complaint can be passed by them. However, they must record the reasons in writing for doing so.

Each one of us is a consumer in some form or another. More often than not, we come across either goods or services in our daily lives. We have a right to quality goods and services and a remedy to enforce the said right in case of any defect or deficiency.

2
Partnership

1. The topics discussed in this chapter relate to certain questions which arise in day-to-day business matters. This discussion is intended to guide the reader to appreciate these questions by a practical approach to a particular query which arises at a given point of time.

2. The topics which give rise to these questions are briefly dealt with here. To better appreciate the discussion, it is necessary to divide the topics as under:

   (i) what is meant by Partnership?

   (ii) goodwill.

   (iii) points to be borne in mind while preparing a Partnership Agreement.

   (iv) liabilities of a partner.

   (v) dissolving a firm and the consequences.

   (vi) difference between Co-ownership and Partnership

   (vii) minors.

3. The word *Note* appears at some places to convey the meaning without a separate discussion.

I. PARTNERSHIP

(a) A Partnership is a contract between two or more persons who can legally place their money, labour and skills in lawful commerce or business to share the profits and bear the losses in certain proportions as recorded in the Partnership (Agreement). The word "legally" means a person who is legally (lawfully) competent to enter into contracts.

(b) The words "Legally Competent" and "Lawful Commerce", require clarification. Competent means that a minor (under the age of 18) cannot legally enter into a contract. Also, a person who is a major but, for instance, suffers from unsoundness of mind is also not competent to contract and cannot legally enter into a contract.

Lawful Commerce means that a partnership has to be formed for a purpose not forbidden by law or which is not against public policy or if the number of partners exceeds 19.

■ Example {for (b)}: Manilal (who is competent to contract) enters into a contract of partnership to procure and sell examination papers with Ratan, a minor (14) and Gandalal who is a major but who is not competent to contract as he suffers from unsoundness of mind.

This contract is illegal because:

(a) Ratan is a minor.
(b) Gandalal is of unsound mind.
(c) Procuring and selling examination papers is forbidden by law.

An important consequence of an illegal partnership is that in the given case, Manilal has acted fraudulently. Ratan and Gandalal are unaware of this illegality. They are entitled to recover damages from Manilal through their respective guardians.

II. GOODWILL

(a) Goodwill is easy to describe but difficult to define. It is the benefit and advantage of a good name, reputation and connection of business. Goodwill is a property and is capable of transfer and is only attached to business.

(b) For example, firms Gordon and Co., or M/s. Reliance Goods or M/s. Tribhovandas enjoy invaluable goodwill. In case of a dispute between the partners that is followed by dissolution, the price factor plays a dominant role and that is why a Partnership Agreement contains an arbitration clause to resolve the dispute on valuation and transfer of goodwill through intervention of well-wishers, without undue publicity.

(c) It is in this context that the Goodwill forms part of the Partnership Agreement as indicated below to minimize disputes on valuation and transfer.

This also reduces the volume of controversy.

III. POINTS TO BE INCLUDED IN A PARTNERSHIP AGREEMENT

(a) Names and addresses of the partners
(b) Name of the firm
(c) Nature of business
(d) Date of commencement and address of the partnership business
(e) Name of the bank/s
(f) Contribution(s) towards capital or loan(s) at an agreed rate of interest permitted under the Income Tax Act
(g) Partners to be entitled to remuneration (salary) as per the limit prescribed by Section 40 (b) (v) of the Income Tax Act

NOTE : This is important because remuneration (salary) is an allowable deduction from the firm's gross income.

(h) Drawings on an agreed basis
(i) Division of Profits and Losses after deducting revenue expenditure

NOTE : The following clauses will minimize disputes if any, as the agreement will prevail.

(a) Death will dissolve the firm so far as concerns the deceased. The survivor(s) will be entitled to continue in the same subject to accounts being made. Goodwill is not to be taken into account.
(b) A partner may retire by giving three months written notice. The firm will be dissolved so far as concerns the retiring partner. The continuing partners will continue.
(c) The firm may be dissolved with three months' written notice. On dissolu-

tion, each party is entitled to carry on the same business separately but by law, with the same name or in a name which sounds like the name of the dissolved firm.

(d) Goodwill to be excluded for accounts or the alternative goodwill to be according to the average of the income for the previous three years. No goodwill in case of dissolution before three years.

(e) Employment of staff by consent.

(f) Partners shall be just and faithful to each other.

(g) Financial year to be April 1 to March 31.

(h) All the partnership disputes to be referred to arbitration under the Arbitration and Conciliation Act, 1996. Each partner to appoint an arbitrator and as joint arbitrators to appoint a third arbitrator (or a common arbitrator). Arbitration is therefore a precondition to seeking relief in a Court.

NOTE: The partners shall register the firm simultaneously with the Registrar of Firms by signing and filing the necessary forms and documents. This is important because an unregistered firm is not under the law, entitled to sue.

■ Example : The (unregistered) firm of Bombay Publishers and Co., is entitled to receive an admitted amount of Rs. three lakhs from Rishabhbhai. The partners of the firm cannot sue Rishabhbhai because the firm is unregistered.

Register the firm with the proper ward of the Income Tax office.

IV. LIABILITY OF PARTNERS

The liability of partners of a firm is joint and individual for an act of the firm.

■ Example : A holder of a valid promissory note executed by one of the partners of the firm (on behalf of the firm) has a right to hold all the partners liable.

V. DISSOLVING A FIRM

(a) Dissolving a firm when the partners have differences between themselves that cannot be settled.

(b) This is the reason why the terms of the Partnership Agreement are important because it must contain an important condition stating that any part-

.ner can purchase the name of the firm by paying an agreed price to the other partner(s).

(c) If there is no agreement, then the court alone has the power to dissolve the firm on the happening of certain events. The consequences include :

   (1) taking of accounts.
   (2) valuation of assets and goodwill.
   (3) arbitration.

NOTE: It would bear mention here that in an emergency, the law also authorizes a partner to take action as he considers fit to protect the firm from loss just as a reasonable person would do in his own case in a similar emergency. This authority however, does not permit the removal of a partner and/or dissolution of the firm.

VI. CO-OWNERSHIP AND PARTNERSHIP

Co-ownership means when property is held jointly by two or more persons, each having a transferable right to the extent of his share. The distinction between co-ownership and partnership was once a disputed issue particularly with relation to dissolution. The Supreme Court has set at rest this controversy by holding that :

(1) co-ownership is not necessarily the result of an agreement, whereas partnership is.

(2) co-ownership does not necessarily involve profit or loss, but partnership does.

(3) one co-owner can, without the permission of the other, transfer his interest etc. to a stranger, a partner cannot do this; and lastly,

(4) while in a partnership each partner acts for all the partners, in a co-ownership one co-owner is not as such the agent of the other.

VII. MINORS

(a) A person under the age of 18 is a minor. The question which usually arises is that if a minor is not capable to enter into a contract, then is it legal to

Partnership

admit him as a partner?

(b) Therefore it would be appropriate to discuss the point of minors being admitted to the benefits of partnership.

(c) A minor can be admitted to the benefits of partnership by consent of all the partners.

(d) A minor is liable for the act of the firm to the extent of his share, but the minor is not personally liable for any such act.

(e) The minor on becoming a major has the option to *elect* to become or not become a partner, by giving the following notices of such election only once:

   (a) to the Registrar of Firms
   (b) in the official gazette
   (c) in any vernacular newspaper where the firm has its principal place of business.

(f) This option has to be exercised within six months of the minor attaining majority or obtaining knowledge that he was admitted as a partner whichever is later/earlier.

(g) If he fails to give such notice he becomes a partner on the expiry of this period of six months.

■ Example: Arjun is a minor. Bharatbhai and Rameshbhai are partners of Reliance and Co. The partners admit Arjun to the benefits of the firm giving him a 7% share in the profits. Rustom files a suit against the firm and its partners including Arjun, to recover an admitted sum of Rs. three lakhs with interest. Arjun's liability would be limited to 7% while he was a minor. However, on majority, he failed to give any notice as per (e) and (f) above, and became a partner by operation of law. Rustom's suit was decided thereafter. The court passed an order for payment in favour of Rustom, by which time, Arjun had become a major. Hence he too became liable as one of the partner's, to pay the ordered amount to Rustom as he had a joint liability from the date on which he was admitted to the benefits of partnership.

The purpose of a partnership agreement is that two or more parties agree to carry on business on the terms recorded in the agreement. The underlying importance of a partnership is that the rights and liabilities of the partners are crystallized and each one has to discharge and conduct himself within the framework of the duties assigned to him in the agreement. A partnership agreement may be termed as a sort of a permanent document with the object of the partners contributing to the growth of the firm. Sometimes, the terms may appear strict but in the longer run it prevents disputes and Arbitration helps in solving them.

DEED OF PARTNERSHIP

THIS DEED OF PARTNERSHIP made at _____ on the _____ day of _____ 200__ BETWEEN (1) SRT of _____, Indian Inhabitant, having address at _____ (which expression shall unless it be repugnant to the context or meaning thereof, include his heirs, executors, administrators, legal representatives and assigns) hereinafter called the Party of the **FIRST PART**; (2) SMG of _____, Indian Inhabitant, having address at _____ (which expression shall unless it be repugnant to the context or meaning thereof, include his heirs, executors, administrators, legal representatives and assigns) hereinafter called the Party of the **SECOND PART.**

WHEREAS

The parties hereto are desirous of carrying on business of _____ in partnership upon the terms and conditions recorded hereinafter.

IT IS HEREBY AGREED BY AND BETWEEN THE PARTIES AS UNDER:

1. The Partnership shall commence on the _____ day of _____ 200__.
2. The name of the firm shall be "Messrs _____".
3. The Partnership shall be "at Will".

4. The business of the Partnership shall be carried on at _____ or at such other place or places as the partners may agree upon.

5. The business of the partnership shall be of _____ _____ and/or such other business as the partners may decide.

6. The accounting year of the partnership shall be from 1st April to 31st March of the next year.

7. The Bankers of the Partnership shall be such bank or banks as the partners may from time to time agree upon and such bank account or accounts shall be operated by such partners or partner as the parties hereto may from time to time agree upon.

8. The capital of the partnership shall be the sum of Rs. _____ /- and shall be provided by the partners in their profit and loss sharing ratio. If at any time hereafter any further capital is required for the purpose of the partnership the same shall, unless otherwise agreed, be contributed by the partners in the same ratio. The partners shall be entitled to interest on the capital brought in by them.

9. Simple interest at the rate of 12% per annum shall be payable on the amounts standing to the credit of Accounts of the Partners, from time to time.

10. The share of the Partners in the profit and loss of the partnership, after payment of interest on Partners' account and remuneration to the Partner, shall be as follows:

    NAMES PERCENTAGE

    (1) SRT

    (2) SMG

11. Proper books of account shall be maintained and be properly posted up and kept at the principal place of business of the partnership or such other place/s as may be agreed upon.

12. Each partner shall:
    (a) devote his whole time and attention to the Partnership business;
    (b) punctually pay and discharge his separate debts and engagements and indemnify the other partners and the partnership assets against the same and all proceedings cost, claims or demands in respect thereof;
    (c) be just and faithful to the other partners in all transactions relating to the partnership business and at all times give to the others a true account of all such dealings.
13. None of the partners shall without the consent of the other Partners:
    (a) engage or be concerned or interested either directly or indirectly in any other similar business or occupation;
    (b) make any contract with or dismiss any employee;
    (c) forgo the whole or any part of any debt or sum due to the partners;
    (d) except in the ordinary course of trade dispose of by loan pledge, sale or otherwise of any part of the partnership property;
    (e) assign or charge their interest in the firm or;
    (f) draw or accept or endorse any bill of exchange or promissory note on account of the partnership.
14. Death of any of the partners hereto shall not dissolve the partnership but the legal representatives of the deceased partner shall be taken up as a partner in place and stead of the deceased partner.
15. The rights, powers, duties and obligations of the parties (partners) hereto shall be governed by The Indian Partnership Act, 1932 or such other statutory modifications or re-enactment thereof.
16. If any dispute arises between the parties hereto in respect of the partnership, the same shall be referred to the Arbitration under The Arbitration and Conciliation Act, 1996 or the Arbitration Act as may be in force.

IN WITNESS WHEREOF the parties hereto have hereunto set and subscribed their respective hands the day and year first hereinabove written.

SIGNED AND DELIVERED by the)
withinnamed, SRT the Party of the First Part,)
in the presence of. ..)

SIGNED AND DELIVERED by the)
withinnamed, SMG the Party of the Second)
Part, in the presence of. ..)

3

Competency To Contract

The concept of contract has been in existence for centuries. With the progress that man and machine have made, the word contract has assumed significance in all fields, ranging from business to marriage. The divide is wide but the underlying principle of a contract remains the same.

1. WHAT IS A CONTRACT?

A contract is an agreement between parties whereby one party promises to do or to not do, a particular thing for the other party. A contract may be either written (i.e. where the terms of the contract are recorded in writing) or oral (i.e. verbal).

A brief explanation here would be proper, which can be summarized as under :

(a) an agreement is a promise or a set of promises.

(b) next follows an offer and the acceptance of that offer.

(c) the consideration of the agreement i.e. what is one party to the agreement willing to do for the other and vice-versa.

3. Therefore, when parties (to a contract) agree (either orally or in writing) to be lawfully bound by mutual promises (made by each other), a contract comes into existence.

■ Example (of an oral contract):

(a) Rohit, an executive in a multinational company, engages a taxi at place

"A" to go to place "B". Rohit sits in the taxi — as soon as the taxi driver downs the meter the contract begins.

(b) So many things have happened in less than a minute.

(c) Rohit made an offer to the taxi driver to take him to place "B". He sat in the taxi and the taxi driver downed the meter i.e. the taxi driver accepted Rohit's offer. The promise is that Rohit will pay to the taxi driver the taxi fare on reaching place "B" and the taxi driver will take Rohit to place "B" and get paid.

All the requirements of a contract are present in this case.

4. WHO IS COMPETENT TO ENTER INTO A CONTRACT?

Any person who is a major according to the Indian Majority Act, 1875 or who is 18 years of age and not disqualified by law on account of insanity (mental imbalance) is competent to enter into a contract. At the same time, such a person must also qualify according to the law governing him, to enter into a contract. A criminal (in jail) is not prohibited by law from entering into a contract.

■ Example : Rakesh is nearly 6 feet tall. He is only 16 years old but looks 20. His uncle Sumanlal makes a contract with Rakesh and appoints him as an agent to do business for him (Sumanlal). Rakesh defrauds a businessman, Shevaram. On a claim from Shevaram, Sumanlal cannot defend himself by saying that his own contract of agency with minor Rakesh is void since he (Sumanlal) was aware that Rakesh was a minor. Further, Shevaram had no means of knowing that Rakesh was a minor.

5. CAPACITY OF A MARRIED WOMAN TO ENTER INTO A CONTRACT

With the progress in society, women, especially married women are more aware of their rights to enter into a contract and also of their rights as wives.

The law permits a married woman to enter into a contract in her own name or as her husband's authorized agent. This is binding on the husband. However, she cannot bind her husband without his authority. In such a case, she is liable to the extent of her *stridhana* (i.e her individual property howsoever acquired and which she has full power to deal with, as she likes).

■ Examples :

(a) Amladevi (27), wife of Rajkumar (29), started her own business of selling sarees. In the course of her business, she sold sarees to a party called Mohanlal. During her dealings with him, Mohanlal filed a claim against Amladevi for defective sarees.

In this case, since Amladevi has entered into a contract of her own accord and in her own right, she is personally liable. Her husband Rajkumar does not come into the picture at all.

(b) Rajkumar appoints his wife Amladevi as his authorized agent to sell television sets.

In case of any claim made against Amladevi, Rajkumar (her husband) will be liable since he is bound by his wife's acts as agent.

However, if Amladevi sells television sets without the authority of her husband, then she alone will be liable.

6. Having dealt with the topics of the rights of married women, it is necessary to discuss briefly certain equally important topics like the following and their effect on a contract.

(a) Insanity
(b) Insolvency
(c) Fraud

A. INSANITY

This is a very sensitive term. Before discussing its legal implications it is necessary to know its meaning. Insanity is an unsound frame of mind, wherein the intellect is deranged. In other words, the person affected by insanity cannot distinguish between right and wrong. The law protects such persons. It is an established principle of law that a contract made by a lunatic or insane person is void.

■ Example: Ratibai, the wife of a lunatic, Gandalal signed a Sale Deed on behalf of Gandalal without obtaining the permission of the court under the Lunacy Act, 1912. The court intervened and held that without the court's permission, the sale deed was unenforceable and void because the lunatic was protected by law.

B. INSOLVENCY

An insolvent is a person who cannot pay his debts in full. Insolvency is a *state*, Failure is an *act* flowing out of that state and Bankruptcy is an *effect* of that act.

Insolvency is thus, a condition of not being able to pay one's debts.

When a trader cannot pay his debts in the ordinary course of business he is in insolvent circumstances. It must be noted that insolvency is a social stigma because no prudent person will do business with such (insolvent) person. This is one aspect of insolvency. The other is the legal angle. Let us again take a simple example of a contract and its performance.

■ Example: Sheth Hakamchand (once a prominent businessman), was declared an insolvent by a court order. Before the passing of the order, he had agreed to sell to Asoomalji, goods worth Rs. five lakh. After the court order was passed, Hakamchand informed Asoomalji that the court had declared him insolvent. Asoomalji was therefore, absolved from buying the goods or from making any payment to Hakamchand.

If, in this case, Asoomalji had made an advance payment to Sheth Hakamchand, then he will be able to recover the same from the estate of Sheth Hakamchand.

C. FRAUD

The word fraud itself indicates something illegal. Let us examine a contract based on fraudulent misrepresentation.

Nowadays, parents are apprehensive to give their consent to their children for an arranged marriage. The apprehension being of what would happen if certain facts regarding the other party, (which should have been disclosed to them), are not disclosed and knowing which, would have discouraged them from entering into the contract of marriage. This is a case of fraud and the aggrieved party can apply to the Court for annulling the marriage.

■ Example: Ratankumar (25), is an executive in a multinational company. He draws a salary of Rs.50,000/- per month and is suffering from a serious and incurable disease. He is soon to be married to Ritakumari (21). Neither he nor his family have disclosed the fact of the disease to Ritukumari, or her family members before arranging their marriage or any time thereafter. This non-disclosure or concealment amounts to a fraud.

The legal consequences of this situation was that Ritukumari applied to the court for annulment of her marriage. The court passed a decree of nullity in her favour after proof of concealment of Ratankumar's (i.e. her husband's) serious and incurable disease before or after the marriage.

Our entire life is based on contracts. Right from moral contracts (with family members and friends) to legally enforceable obligations, a contract plays a significant role in our lives. We have seen the formation of a contract and the competency of a person to enter into a contract. We have also discussed a contract made by a married woman and the relation of agency she shares with her husband. We have seen the effect of fraud on a contract.

4

Indemnity & Guarantee

1. Having discussed the personal side of a contract let us take a look at contracts which are signed in the course of business. The following matters arise when parties enter into business transactions.

   (a) Indemnity and Guarantee
   (b) Bank Guarantee
   (c) Surety and Guarantor's liability
   (d) Continuing Guarantee

2. Before discussing (a) above, it is necessary to explain the meaning of each term. Comprehension and application will then be easy.

INDEMNITY AND GURANTEE

(i) Indemnity is something which one person (for example "A") agrees to give to another ("B") in the event of any loss, which may be caused to the other person ("B"). The loss may be caused by an act of the party giving the indemnity (i.e. "A"), or by an act of another person. This is a contract of indemnity. The person giving the indemnity is the *indemnifier* and the party in whose favour or for whose benefit an indemnity is given is the *indemnified* person. Indemnity is thus, a formal legal acceptance (by the indemnifier) of responsibility against damage or loss (caused to the person indemnified). Let us take a simple illustration.

■ Example: Robin is the seller of a flat and John is the purchaser. Robin gives a written assurance (i.e. an indemnity) to John that if he, John, suffers any loss on account of any misrepresentation by Robin in the sale deed of the flat (such as a defect in Robin's title to the flat) then Robin will indemnify John against such loss. Robin will also be liable to make good the loss suffered by John if a third party makes a claim that there is a valid agreement for sale between Robin and him in respect of the same flat.

(ii) Guarantee: A contract of guarantee is a contract by which one person promises to pay the obligation of another. It is a promise to answer for the payment of some debt, or the performance of some duty, in case of the failure of another party, who is in the first instance liable for such payment or performance. The person who gives the guarantee is known as the *guarantor* or the *surety*. The person in respect of whose default the guarantee is given is called the *principal debtor*. The person to whom the guarantee is given is called the *creditor*. A guarantee may be oral or written.

■ Example: Rustomji introduces his friend Byramji to another friend Cawasji to arrange a loan transaction of Rs. 3 lakh between Byramji and Cawasji. Both Byramji and Cawasji are not known to each other. Cawasji advances Rs. three lakh to Byramji at interest on Rustomji's agreeing in writing, to make good the payment to Cawasji , if Byramji defaults.

(i) Rustomji is the guarantor of the loan given by Cawasji to Byramji

(ii) Byramji is the principal debtor

(iii) Cawasji is the creditor (i.e the person who is to receive the money).

BANK GURANTEE

This is a guarantee given by a bank to pay or repay, a specified sum in the event of any default in performance by the principal debtor of some other contract with a third party, the creditor. The bank, at the request of its customer issues a guarantee. This document enables the customer to perform his trade smoothly.

A bank guarantee is of two types: *conditional* and *unconditional.*

A conditional bank guarantee is one where the guarantor becomes liable to the party claiming under the guarantee, when the breach of contract or the loss occuring from there or both have been proved. In an unconditional bank guarantee, as the name suggests, the guarantor is bound immediately, from the moment the principal debtor fails to perform his contract. It is the obligation of the bank to honour an unconditional bank guarantee, as per its terms.

SURETY OR GUARANTOR'S LIABILITY

A contract of guarantee comes into existence when there is a liability. This is the liability of the principal debtor. The liability of the guarantor is co-extensive with that of the principal debtor when there is no limit on the extent of liability of the principal debtor. The extent of liability of the guarantor otherwise will depend on the terms of the contract of guarantee. A creditor cannot be prevented from taking action against the guarantor on the ground that the principal is financially sound or that the creditor may have some remedy against the principal debtor in some other proceedings.

Further, the liability of a guarantor does not, in all cases arise simultaneously with that of the principal debtor. A guarantor would be liable where he had contracted to remain liable although the principal debtor may have been discharged. In other words, it means that even if the principal debtor is discharged, the guarantor's liability would still continue. Alternatively, a guarantor's liability by a contract, will arise only after the creditor has exercised all his rights and remedies available against the principal debtor and has failed to recover any amount from him.

■ Example: Raman takes a loan of Rs. 67 lakh from Ratan. Kanchanlal stands as a guarantor for the repayment of the loan by Raman to Ratan, subject to a contract that Ratan will first use all remedies available to him in law against Raman before enforcing the guarantee against Kanchanlal.

This example has been discussed in detail in a High Court case.

CONTINUING GUARANTEE

A guarantee which extends to a series of transactions is known as a *continuing guarantee*.

The distinction between an ordinary and a continuing guarantee is important with reference to the duration of the liability of the guarantor/surety. In an ordinary guarantee, the surety is liable only in respect of a single transaction. Under a continuing guarantee, the surety is prima facie liable in respect of any of the successive transactions which come within its scope, unless it is revoked.

■ Example: Milwala supplies synthetic yarn to Patrawala on a running account basis. Reshamwala guarantees payment to Milwala to the tune of Rs. 25 lakh for the synthetic yarn which Milwala may supply to Patrawala from time to time. Milwala supplies yarn to Patrawala worth Rs. ten lakh and Patrawala pays for the same. Milwala once again supplies yarn to Patrawala for Rs. 20 lakh, but this time the buyer (Patrawala) fails to pay for the same. Reshamwala's guarantee, which is a continuing guarantee is thus invoked and he is liable to pay to Milwala (the seller), to the tune of Rs. 25 lakh as the amount guaranteed by him.

One must remember that the guarantor's liability is not more than the guaranteed amount. When a guarantee is obtained by misrepresentation or by the creditor or with his knowledge and consent relating to a material part of the transaction the same is not valid. Therefore, a guarantor or a surety is discharged from liability in the event of a fraud

---

FORMAT OF AN INDEMNITY

INDEMNITY

We, (1) _____, (2) _____,
(3) _____ all adults, Indian Inhabitants, of _____ residing at _____ hereby declare that:

1. By an Agreement dated ..... we purchased property bearing flat no. ____, _____ floor, _____ from .... Builders/Vendors.

2. A Society viz.: _____ of the flat owners has been formed. However, we have been informed by the Society that the Share certificate has not been issued so far and will be issued at a later date.

3. We undertake to handover the Share Certificate to _____ as on receiving the same.

4. At the request of _____, we confirm having agreed to keep indemnifying _____ and permanently indemnified against any claim which may be made by any third party or any loss suffered and in respect of all costs charges and expenses incurred in respect of any matter touching the said Agreement and also in respect of any matter directly or indirectly touching the non issue of Share Certificate.

Solemnly declared by

(i) _____,

(ii) _____,

(iii) _____.

Witness:

5

Negotiable Instruments

The reader will have noticed that the discussion in the preceding chapters have centered around commerce, trade or day-to-day business, how contracts are made etc.

One of the most important features of the commercial world is a negotiable instrument.

1. What is an Instrument?

   One must know that the law governing Negotiable Instruments is universal. In other words, it is the law of the business community. The finer details may differ from nation to nation but the essentials have remained static. Courts are giving due weightage to the concept of socio-economic justice and are adapting a more pragmatic meaning to the law of Negotiable Instruments in the large interest of the business community to meet the legitimate demands of the present.

2. A Negotiable Instrument is a promissory note or a bill of exchange or a cheque, payable either to the bearer of the Instrument or to the order. As long as there are no words prohibiting transfer or *not transferable* is endorsed on the instrument, it is negotiable.

3. The definition consists of different parts. It is therefore necessary to give examples along with the explanation.

4. (a) Promissory Note : It is a promise to pay on demand, a certain amount of money only to, or to the order of a certain person, or to the bearer

of the instrument.

Sample: On demand I promise to pay to Rajkumar Lakhandas a sum of Rs. 2,00,000/- (Rupees Two Lakh only) in Bombay with interest at 12% per annum for value received in Bombay.

Bombay dated this 5th day of April, 2004.
Bharatkumar Ramanlal
Promisor

(b) (i) The words "on demand" and "promise" are self-explanatory.

    (ii) The words "in Bombay" and Bombay dated....." are important. The same consider that payment receipt and promise to pay and signing have all taken place in Bombay. Therefore Courts in Bombay alone will have jurisdiction to entertain any claim based on the above Promissory Note.

    (iii) There are two parties to a Promissory Note, the *promisor* and the *promisee*.

5. Bill of Exchange: A Bill of Exchange is an instrument in writing containing an unconditional order. It is signed by the maker (of the Bill) directing a certain person to pay a certain sum of money only to, or to the order, of a certain person or to the bearer of the instrument.

Sample :

New Delhi
1st October, 2004

On demand pay to Mr. C. Ramchandran or order the sum of Rupees Seventy Thousand only.

S. Balakrishnan
New Delhi

To
Mr. Gopal Menon
14, Esplanade
Chennai (Madras)
T.N.

Note : These few lines communicate so much information.

(i) The drawer Balakrishnan is New Delhi based.

The holder is Ramchandran.

Menon is a Chennai based drawee.

(ii) The Bill is a direction to Menon to pay to Ramchandran in Chennai Rs.70,000/- when Ramchandran presents the Bill to Menon for payment.

6. Cheque: Even a minor is familiar with the word Cheque. Yet the discussions which follow will explain that a cheque is not as simple as one would consider it. A cheque is a vital document.

   (i) It is important to note that a cheque is a Bill of Exchange drawn on a specific bank and not expressed to be payable otherwise than on demand. It also includes a truncated (shortened) cheque and a cheque in the electronic form (i.e. an exact mirror image of a paper cheque)

   (ii) A truncated cheque is one which is made smaller in size during the course of clearing cycle immediately on generation of an electronic image.

   ■ Example: Rohit Mithaiwala draws a cheque for Rs.50,000/- on Central Bank, Fort Branch, Bombay in favour of Ramesh Shah. The bank will honour the cheque on demand by Ramesh. The cheque also includes the mirror image of the cheque. This cheque is then put for clearing and gets shortened in size by cutting in the clearing house.

   The same cheque has thus gone through three stages :

   (a) Presentation for clearance.

   (b) Getting a mirror image.

   (c) Shortening of the cheque by cutting in the clearing house.

   (iii) A post-dated cheque is one, which contains a future date than the date of its delivery. Legally, it is immaterial whether a cheque is ante-dated or post-dated. It is still payable on presentment at anytime on and after the date mentioned on it.

(IV) Crossing of Cheques : When two transverse lines are put across the face of the cheque, it is known as crossing of a cheque. A crossed cheque is a direction to the banker not to pay the cheque across the counter but to pay only to a banker thereby affording protection to the owner of the cheque.

All the cheque types are honoured as long as the drawer has enough funds in his account.

7. This brings us to another feature called Consideration. There is a presumption in law that every negotiable instrument was made or drawn for consideration until the contrary is proved. It is important to note that before the presumption is drawn, the execution or signing of the instrument must be admitted or proved.

■ Example: Rustomji executed a promissory note dated January 12, 2004 on his letter head in favour of Sohrabji for Rs three lakh payable at Delhi. Following Rustomji's failure to pay any part of the promised amount on demand to Sohrabji, Sohrabji filed a suit in court against Rustomji on the unpaid promissory note. Sohrabji proved the execution of the promissory note in court. Once the execution of the promissory note was proved, the court was bound to raise a presumption that consideration had passed.

This discussion explains that when a promissory note/Bill of Exchange is drawn, it is presumed that the consideration has passed. The meaning of the words "until otherwise proved" casts an obligation on the promisee (i.e. the person in whose favour the promissory note is given) only to prove execution. Once that is done the presumption becomes foolproof and definite.

6

Trusts

There are many people who are keen to donate property for the benefit of needy and deserving persons. Very often they do not know how to go about doing so. Charitable Trusts are bodies specifically set up for these purposes.

1. MEANING

A charitable trust is one, which is created for the benefit of unascertained, uncertain and sometimes, a fluctuating body of individuals, in which the beneficiary may be a portion or class of a public community, eg, persons who are AIDS victims or for the benefit, such as for the education of poor children of a particular caste or community.

Since a charitable trust is intended to benefit the needy and deserving, a person may use his own property for the purposes of forming a charitable trust.

2. PUBLIC TRUST

A public trust is an express or constructive trust for public or charitable purposes or both. It includes a temple, a *muth*, a church or any other place of worship. It also includes a society formed for religious or philanthropic purposes.

A charitable purpose includes medical aid, shelter homes and education.

■ Example: Samaaj Seva Charitable Trust was set up for the purpose of providing free education to the students of a special learning school. However, for some reasons, the school was forced to close down. Since the main objective of the Trust was to provide education to handicapped children, it was possible to use the funds of the Trust for a similar purpose, for another school.

3. TRANSFER OF PROPERTY TO A TRUST

In relation to *moveable property,* the ownership of the property can be transferred by a physical act of handing over its possession to the trust.

An *immovable property* may be transferred to the Trust by a Will or a Deed of Trust. The title of the property should be clear and marketable.

■ Example: Arindam Chatterjee, is 86 years old. He has several properties in his name (both moveable and immoveable) but has no heirs. In his Will he states that three of his flats on Park Street, Calcutta be transferred to Kar Bhala Charitable Trust. This is a valid method of transfer of property in the name of the Trust.

4. PRIVATE TRUST

The provisions relating to a private trust are governed by the Indian Trusts Act, 1882.

In a private family trust, the author (i.e the person who creates the trust) is the Settlor, and he is the owner of the property.

Role of Trustees:

A. Duties and Rights include :

  (i) a trustee is bound to fulfill the purpose of the trust and to obey the direction of the Settlor.
  (ii) a trustee must acquaint himself with the trust property (both moveable and immoveable) and invest the trust money in securities.

(iii) a trustee is bound to keep proper accounts of the trust.

(iv) a trustee must prosecute or defend legal claims/proceedings by or against the trust.

(v) when a trustee has been empowered to sell the trust property, he also has the power to insert stipulations in the transaction and also has power to cancel the agreement for sale.

■ Example: Bankelal was appointed trustee of Krishnamoorthy Trust. He was authorized by the trust deed to sell their property in Uran. During the negotiations, the purchasers of the property requested Bankelal to sell them the property at a rate lower than the market value and offered him a commission. Bankelal terminated the contract.

B. Disabilities

(i) A trustee is not entitled to remuneration for the time spent and the trouble taken by him in executing the trust.

(ii) A trustee must utilize the trust funds for the objects of the trust and nothing else.

■ Example: Danny Gonsalves, was appointed trustee of Care Well Trust. At the same time, he was a partner in an export firm. Since the firm was not doing well financially, he withdrew a substantial some of money from the trust's bank account to revive his firm. He was liable to account for the loss to the beneficiary.

5. COMPANIES ACT

A charitable trust can also be set up as a company. Such a company is formed for charitable purposes, for promoting commerce, arts, science, religion or similar objects and applies its profits or income for the promotion of such purposes. It has no liability as that of a company although it enjoys all the privileges available to companies under the Indian Companies Act.

Charitable trusts serve as a link between the prosperous and the needy in society. However, the management of the charitable trusts must be in safe hands. A person should not derive a benefit from the trust for an individual or self-serving purpose.

Power Of Attorney

A Power of Attorney is an authority given by one person to another, to do the acts specified in the power on his behalf.

MEANING

A Power of Attorney is a document creating an authority. It creates a relationship of principal and agent between a person giving the power (i.e. principal) to another to act on his behalf as agent. It is a very serious document and must be given with maximum care.

■ Examples:

(i) Haridas Kadam executes a Power of Attorney in favour of Rajan Shah to do everything necessary to sell his property since Kadam travels frequently.

(ii) Sabrina Electronics Limited, after a decision of the Board of Directors executed a Power of Attorney in favour of its Director Mr. Shudhanshu Mukherjee to represent the company in a case they intended to file against Mr. Chaterjee.

TYPES OF POWER OF ATTORNEY

A Power of Attorney may be either General or Special.

- General - A general Power of Attorney is a wide-ranging and broad power covering a large number of matters. A general power is really a power to do

Power Of Attorney

anything legal which the donor of the power would have done.

- **Example**: Hansaben will be traveling abroad for a year. She appoints Girdharilal as her attorney and executes a Power of Attorney in his favour, to look after her flat and other properties, pay all necessary bills, operate her bank accounts, look after her business etc. and generally, to do all things on her behalf. This is a general wide ranging power given to Girdharilal.
- Special - A special power is a power relating to a precise subject matter accompanied with a power to do a number of other acts in relation to that power.
- **Example**: Thomas Henderson executes a Power of Attorney to Das Babu, to attend to his legal matter in court. For this purpose, Das Babu has the power to sign legal documents, appoint/change lawyers etc.

DELEGATION OF AUTHORITY

A Power of Attorney is, in effect, an *entrustment* of authority by the donor of the power, in favour of the other.

A power of attorney is also executed when a specialist is required for a particular job to be done. For instance, a litigant appoints a lawyer to represent him in the Civil Court, in his matter.

REVOCATION

A Power of Attorney can be revoked by the donor/principal, if:

(i) the purpose for which the power is given gets fulfilled or comes to an end.

(ii) the principal dies or becomes insane or is adjudged insolvent.

(iii) it is revoked by the donor unless the power is irrevocable.

- **Example**: Karimbhai executes a Power of Attorney in favour of Abbas for collecting rent on his behalf from his tenants, for the year 2003. Once the year is over, the power in favour of Abbas stands revoked.

VALIDATION OF POWER

For its legal validity, a Power of Attorney must be signed in the presence of a court, judge or a public notary. If the area within which the power is to be executed is a metropolitan area, then it can be signed before a Metropolitan Magistrate and when it is outside a metropolitan area, then before a Judicial Magistrate.

No Power of Attorney has legal sanctity unless it is authenticated by any of the above mentioned persons. A Power of Attorney can be given by more than one person in favour of another, regarding the same or separate transactions. It is not compulsory to register a Power of Attorney under the Indian Registration Act. A power of attorney given for the purposes of development of immoveable property is liable for stamp duty as a conveyance since it creates interest in immoveable property in Maharashtra.

SPECIMEN OF A SPECIAL POWER OF ATTORNEY

(This is a special power of attorney to give on leave and license residential premises)

TO ALL to whom these presents shall come, I Girdharilal Shah, of Mumbai Indian Inhabitant, residing at Adarsh Nagar, 11th Cross Lane, Mumbai 400 060, SEND GREETINGS:

WHEREAS:

1. I am the Owner of Flat No.214 in Rambha Building, Worli, Mumbai 400 037, ("the said Flat")more particularly described in Schedule "I" hereunder written. The said Flat is lying vacant.

2. As I am of old age, and unable to attend to my day to day affairs, I have authorized Shri Bhanwarlal, residing at A/2 Co-operative Housing Society Ltd. Mulund, Mumbai to contact prospective Licencees for the said Flat.

3. I am, therefore, desirous of appointing Shri Bhanwarlal as my Attorney to give the said Flat on Leave and License basis to a suitable person on my behalf and which the said attorney has agreed to do.

NOW KNOW YOU ALL AND THESE PRESENTS WITNESS that I do hereby nominate, constitute and appoint Shri Bhanwarlal to be my true and lawful Attorney for the purpose expressed that is to say:

1. To look for a suitable Licensee for the said Flat and to give advertisements if necessary and to do all acts and things necessary for effectively finding a suitable Licensee.

2. AND I DO HEREBY agree to ratify and confirm all and whatever my said Attorney shall or purport to do or cause to be done by virtue of these presents.

IN WITNESS WHEREOF I have put my hand this 21st day of February, 2002.

SIGNED AND DELIVERED BY

the withinnamed Girdharilal Shah in

the presence of Firoz Gamadia.

Before The Sub-Registrar

8

Purchase & Sale Of Goods

Meaning

Goods means and includes every kind of moveable property such as stocks, shares, and things attached to the earth which are agreed to be severed before sale, or under the contract of sale. It does *not* include money. Goods are the subject matter of the agreement of sale. Goods may be either existing goods, owned or possessed by the seller, or future goods, such as (i) goods to be manufactured by the seller from material lying with him (ii) goods expected to come into existence e.g. milk from a cow or a new born calf.

A *buyer* of goods is one who buys or agrees to buy goods and a *seller* is one who sells or agrees to sell goods. The consideration which a buyer pays to the seller for the goods, is the *price*.

A *contract* of sale of goods is a contract where the seller transfers (or agrees to transfer) the goods to the buyer for a price.

■ Example: Hexicon Limited enters into an agreement with M/s Furtardo and Sons for purchase of steel. Furtardo and Sons (the seller) sells the goods (i.e. steel) to the company for Rs.1,25,000/- (i.e. the price). This is a contract for sale of goods.

PRICE

The price for goods may be fixed under the contract or as the parties may agree.

Where no price is fixed, the buyer must pay to the seller, a reasonable price (i.e. the prevalent market rate).

■ Example: Kelly Company. Pvt. Ltd. entered into a contract with Buddhibhai and Sons for the purchase of 100 bales of cotton. It was an oral contract. No price was fixed between the parties. At the time of payment, the company paid Buddhibhai and Sons, Rs.10,000/- (i.e. @ Rs 100/- per bale of cotton which was the prevailing market rate at that time).

CONDITION AND WARRANTY

A Condition is a requirement which is "essential" to the main purpose of the contract, the violation of which gives a right to treat the contract as rejected.

When a person contracts with another, he is bound to perform the contract according to its terms.

■ Example: In a contract between Mohammed Asim and Anantkumar Foods, Asim contracted to deliver 100 kgs of potatoes. However, what was actually delivered were onions. This failure on the part of Asim is not merely a breach of one terms of the contract, but in fact, it was a total failure on his part to perform the contract.

A Warranty is a requirement "collateral" to the main purpose of the contract. In case of a breach, it gives a right to claim damages but not a right to refuse the goods and treat the contract as terminated.

■ Example: The newly formed Bilkis Transport Company Limited placed an order with M/s Super Motors for the purchase of three cargo trucks. The money for the same was paid in advance. The company was assured by Super Motors that the trucks will be delivered within 30 days. Accordingly, the company accepted orders for transporting material after a month. However, the trucks were delayed by more than a month. This resulted in a loss of business to the company. In an action filed against Super Motors, the company was successful in prosecuting its claim for damages.

There is no implied condition or warranty with relation to the quality or fitness of any particular purpose of goods in a sale unless the buyer specifically informs the seller, the particular purpose for which he requires the goods – to show that he relies on the skill and judgment of the seller.

Otherwise, the buyer relies on his own skill and judgment when he purchases the goods.

■ Example: Rustam Jeejeebhoy, a veterinary surgeon placed an order for the purchase of an electric razor to be used for cutting animal hair. However, he was, supplied with a razor for human usage. Mr. Jeejeebhoy was entitled to reject the goods.

THE SELLER'S RESPONSIBILITY

In a contract for sale, there is an implied condition by the seller that he has a right to sell the goods and in the case of an agreement to sell, he will have a right to sell the goods and that the buyer will have the right to enjoy the possession of the goods. It is the seller's responsibility that the goods be free from any defect or charge in favour of any other party not known to the buyer.

■ Example: Car Bazaar, a second hand car dealer company had advertised regarding a sale of second hand cars. Mr. Hasmukh purchased a car from the sale. He paid the consideration for the same. He was told that the car papers would be sent to him in a week, after the transfer procedure. However, within a few days he was approached by the law enforcement agencies who stated that his car was in fact, stolen. Mr. Hasmukh, was bound to return the car. He was however, entitled to recover the price of the car from Car Bazaar.

Sale by Description

When there is a contract for sale of goods by Description, it is the seller's responsibility that the goods must correspond with the description. The word description means that the goods could be recognized or identified as the seller had described them to be.

In order for the property in the goods to pass from the buyer to the seller, the goods must be capable of being ascertained.

■ Example: The internet web site of a leading photocopying company had offered a "2003 Machine", in new condition and with original parts. Mr.

Hingorani placed an order for the same, for his shop. When the machine arrived, it was found that the stand was partly broken, the glass was not original and a few switches were not functioning. Mr. Hingorani was entitled to reject the machine since the goods (i.e. the photocopy machine) did not correspond with the description on the web site.

Sale by Sample

In the case of a contract for sale by sample, there is an implied condition that the bulk shall correspond with the sample in quality. The buyer will have a reasonable opportunity to compare the goods. The goods must be free from defect.

■ Example: Hi-Tech Pharmaceuticals Company Limited is an exporter of different kinds of drugs. A concern from U.S.A. placed an order with the company for the purchase of 100 kilograms of a particular drug for animal treatment, after approving the sample. However, when the consignment of 100 kilograms was exported, it was found that the drugs were far inferior in quality and could not be used on animals. The American concern was entitled to reject the goods, as the quality did not match.

GOODS SENT ON 'APPROVAL' OR 'SALE OR RETURN BASIS'

When goods are delivered to the buyer on approval or on sale or return basis, the property passes to the buyer when he communicates his approval to the seller *or* although he does not signify his approval, he retains the goods without rejection for more than reasonable time.

■ Example : Comfort Wear Apparel Store sent on approval, ten T-shirts to their customer. The customer started wearing the t-shirts. It was understood that he had accepted the goods.

RISK

Normally, the goods remain at the seller's risk until the property therein is transferred to the buyer. Once the property is transferred, the goods are at the buyer's risk whether delivery has been made or not.

■ Example: Winnie D'Costa placed an order for the purchase for five boats anchored at Karjat Jetty. She paid half of the total consideration for the five boats and took delivery of two. In the mean time, heavy floods and high tide destroyed the other three boats. The property in the boats had been already transferred to Ms. D'Costa although she had not taken the delivery of all and she was bound to pay the balance money.

DELIVERY OF WRONG QUANTITY

(i) Where the seller delivers to the buyer, goods of a lesser quantity, the buyer may reject them or if he accepts them, must pay for them at the contractual rate.

(ii) If a larger quantity is delivered than what was contracted, the buyer may accept the goods included in the contract and reject the rest or he may simply reject the whole.

■ Example: Jatinder Singh placed an order for five horses, of which three were to be male, and two, female. Instead, five male and five female horses were delivered to him. He was entitled to reject the entire consignment.

UNPAID SELLER

The seller of goods becomes an Unpaid Seller when the entire price has not been paid to him. An unpaid seller has lien on the goods for the price while he is in possession of them despite the fact that the property therein has passed to the buyer. He also has a right to resale. When the buyer is insolvent, the seller has a right to stop the goods in transit.

■ Example: Shreejit Lalchi takes a loan from Any Time Credit Company for the purchase of a motor car. The term for repayment is 24 months. However, Mr. Lalchi becomes insolvent within the second month of the loan. The company is thus entitled to take the car back.

AUCTION SALE

Where goods are put up in lots, for sale in an auction, each lot is a separate contract. The sale is complete when the auctioneer knocks down the hammer.

SUITS FOR BREACH OF CONTRACT

Suit for Price

Where the property in the goods has passed to the buyer and he wrongfully refuses to pay for the goods, the seller may sue him for the price.

■ Example: Raghuvir Metals Limited supplied 25 kilograms of steel to Ravi Kaul. The buyer paid an earnest money deposit for the goods saying that he would make the balance payment on delivery. When the goods were delivered, Kaul failed to make the payment. The company can sue him for price of the goods.

Damages for Non-Acceptance

Where the buyer wrongfully refuses or neglects to take delivery of the goods and pay for them, the seller may sue him for damages for non-acceptance of the goods.

Damages for Non-Delivery

When the seller wrongfully refuses to deliver the goods, the buyer may sue him for non-delivery of the goods.

■ Example: M/s. All Year Fruits, Bombay entered into a contract with Woy Yung Mein from China, for supplying of fresh mangoes. The Bombay based concern was liable for damages to the buyer from China since tthey were unable to supply fresh mangoes in the month of September, as they are not in season.

Thus, we have seen the principles governing sale and purchase of goods in brief. The relevance of conditions and warranties have also been highlighted. The rights of the aggrieved party (such as the unpaid seller) have also been discussed.

9

Principal & Agent

1. MEANING

An Agent is a person who is employed to do any act for another person or to represent such other person, in transactions with third parties. The person for whom *or* on whose behalf such an act is done *or* who is so represented, is called the Principal.

- Any person other than one who is not of the age of maturity or is of unsound mind can become an agent.

  Agency means a relation, which exists wherein one person has an authority (given by the principal) to create a legal relation between the principal and third parties. A relation of agency may be created orally or in writing. Agency is thus a contract. The *test* of the contract of agency is whether the agent who is entering into the transaction on behalf of his principal has the power/authority to create, modify or terminate contractual relationship/s between his principal and third parties.

    - The relationship of agency need not always be contractual. It may arise out of law.

2. CREATION OF THE CONTRACT OF AGENCY

The relation of a principal and agent may be *express* (in writing) or *implied* from the circumstances. An express agency may be in the form of a formal document such as a Power of Attorney given by the principal to his agent, to execute the acts mentioned therein, on his behalf. An express agency can also be created with a letter addressed by the principal specifying the agent's appointment.

On the other hand, an implied agency may be inferred from the conduct or situation of the parties.

■ Example : Goods purchased by Akshay were received by Shobhan, who sold the same to a third party. This is implied agency.

In certain cases of agency, the law prescribes certain requirements to be met, such as a lawyer's appearance in court on behalf of his client, must be with a written document, known as *vakalatnama*.

For instance, a specific power of attorney given on behalf of Ruskin Ltd. to its director, Mr. A.L. Shah, to institute a money suit on behalf of the company, must be given under the common seal of the company and should be accompanied by a Board Resolution.

3. EXTENT OF AGENT'S AUTHORITY

An agent having the principal's authority to execute certain acts, can act within the framework of the authority.

■ Example : Raman Jadeja, appointed Kumar S., as his advocate in a High Court suit that he had filed . The authority includes appearances in court, accepting letters and replying to them. In other words, Kumar S. is authorized to do all things necessary for prosecuting the suit. This authority however, does allow Kumar S. to agree to, for instance, a settlement without his client's (i.e. Mr. Jadeja) signature on the document.

One must remember that agency is not a permanent relationship.

4. WHAT DOES NOT CONSTITUTE AGENCY

The following are certain instances where the relationship of agency is not formed though it may appear to be so:

- the day to day acts of a bank in the course of its business of banking such as payment of bills, debiting accounts, collecting money on behalf of the customer, etc, does not make the bank an agent of the customer.

- when the terms of a contract describe the relationship between the parties as that of principal to principal, it is not a contract of agency although the person is referred to in the contract as agent.

- similarly, advice given by one stockbroker to another in matters of investments, does not make the former an agent of the latter.

- an agent is not a servant but a servant is generally, for some purposes his master's agent. A driver is his master's agent. If the driver while on duty damages another's vehicle, the master is liable to repair the damage.

5. TYPES OF AGENTS

a. General and Special

A general agent is one who has the authority of his principal in all matters concerning the principal or for some act or acts. A General Power of Attorney holder is a general agent. On the other hand, a special agent is appointed for a particular purpose or occasion. The (above) example of Jadeja and Kumar S. applies. Kumar S, is an agent appointed for a particular purpose. When the purpose is served the agency ends.

b. Auctioneer

An auctioneer is a person authorized by law or engaged to sell lands or goods of other persons, at a public auction. He is the agent of the seller. Sometimes, he may be the agent of the buyer *and* seller.

c. Delcredere Agent

A delcredere agent is one who, in exchange for extra remuneration, guarantees the performance of a contract. This factor distinguishes him from other types of agents. This additional remuneration is called delcredere commission. He undertakes to be answerable to his principal for the due performance of the contracts made by him on his behalf. He is not primarily liable to the principal. His liability arises only if the parties with whom he contracts, defaults and in effect, guarantees the principal against losses through their (i.e. the party's) bankruptcy or insolvency.

■ Example: Arun, a delcredere agent in a sale transaction guarantees Vikas (the seller), the receipt of money from Amit (the purchaser). However, Arun will not be accountable to Amit (the purchaser) with regard to Vikas (the seller) performing his part of the contract.

d. Mercantile Agent

A mercantile agent is one who has authority of his principal to sell goods or to buy goods or raise money on the security of goods in the normal course of his business as agent.

e. Director of a Company

A company acts through its directors since it cannot act on its own. Hence, the directors are the agents of the company, on whose behalf they transact the business of the company. On the other hand, the managing director of a company is an employee as well as an agent of the company, depending upon the terms of his employment and the Articles of Association.

f. Others

- The cashier of a shop, who receives money on its behalf and pays its expenses, is an agent of the shop.
- The agent of an insurer, when he fills up an insurance policy for the insured, acts as the agent of the insured.
- When the addressee of a money order requests the sender to send the same by post, the post office becomes the agent of the addressee.

6. DELEGATION OF AGENT'S AUTHORITY

An agent cannot employ another to perform the acts which he has undertaken to perform personally, unless it is necessary to employ a *sub-agent* (i.e. the agent's agent) in the course of business.

A sub-agent acts under the control of the original agent.

The agent is responsible to the principal for the acts of the sub-agent.

7. TERMINATION OF AGENCY

An agency stands terminated if:

(i) the principal revokes his authority.

(ii) the agent renounces the agency.

(iii) the business of the agency is completed.

(iv) the principal is adjudicated insolvent.

(v) if either the principal or the agent dies or becomes of unsound mind.

The termination of an agency determines the authority of the agent and brings an end to the relation between the principal and agent. The agent is however, entitled to receive the remuneration he has earned before the termination.

Part 2
Property Matters

1
Sale

Sale is one of the modes by which ownership of a property is transferred by one party to another. In this chapter, we will discuss the transfer of *immovable property* by way of sale.

What is a sale?

Sale is transfer of ownership of immovable property in consideration for a price. The price can be paid or promised to be paid, or part paid and part promised to be paid.

There is complete transfer of all rights in the property.

Essential elements of sale

- There must be two parties i.e. the seller and the buyer.
- The subject matter is immovable property.
- Transfer of ownership should be for consideration i.e. money.
- Price can be paid or promised to be paid, or partly paid and partly promised.

■ Example : Ajay (The vendor) sold his flat to Vijay (The purchaser) for Rs.10,00,000/-. Ajay has transferred his ownership in the flat to Vijay for the price of Rs.10,00,000/-.

Sale

Vijay can pay Rs.10,00,000/- at one time **or** he can promise to pay Rs. 10,00, 000/- **or** he can pay Rs.5,00,000/- as part payment and can promise to pay the balance Rs. 5,00,000/- at a mutually agreed date. After full payment, Vijay will become the owner of the flat.

RIGHTS OF A BUYER

Before completion of the sale :

(1) A Buyer has a claim on the property for the purchase price paid by him in anticipation of the delivery of the property.
(2) He can claim interest on the purchase price paid by him to the seller.
(3) If the seller fails to transfer the property after the agreement to sell is entered into between him and the buyer, the buyer can file a suit to compel the seller in relation to the specific performance of the contract i.e. to transfer the property to him as agreed upon by them.

After completion of the sale :

The buyer is entitled to the benefit of any increase in the value of the property, as well as any rent arising out of such property.

DUTIES AND LIABILITIES OF THE BUYER

(1) He should pay purchase price to the seller or any person as the seller directs.
(2) When there is an encumbrance on the property, then the buyer may pay the amount of encumbrance (out of the purchase price), to the person who is entitled to the same.

If in the above example, the flat is mortgaged with Bank of India for Rs. 2,00,000/- and the interest amount on the loan is Rs. 2,000, then Vijay can retain Rs. 2,02,000/- to pay to Bank of India and pay the balance Rs. 7,98,000/- to Ajay.

RIGHTS OF A SELLER

Before completion of the sale :
The Seller is entitled to all the rents arising out of the property till the ownership passes to the buyer.

After completion of the sale :
The Seller has a claim on the property which is in the hands of the purchaser, for the unpaid purchase price.

DUTIES AND LIABILITIES OF A SELLER

Before completion of the sale :
(1) to disclose all defects in the property or in his title to the property.
(2) to co-operate with the buyer in completing the sale.

After completion of the sale :
(1) to give possession of the property to the buyer.
(2) the seller must deliver all the documents relating to the property to the buyer after the whole purchase price is paid,

When the property is sold to different buyers, then the purchaser of the greatest value is entitled to retain the (original) documents.

■ Example : X is the owner of four flats viz.:

Flat No. 1 valued at Rs.5,00,000/-

Flat No. 2 valued at Rs.15,00,000/-

Flat No. 3 valued at Rs.20,00,000/- and

Flat No. 4 valued at Rs.40,00,000/-.

All the flats have been purchased by him under one sale deed.

Y purchased flat No. 2 and Z purchased the remaining flats, then Z is entitled to the original sale deed.

SAMPLE

AGREEMENT FOR SALE

THIS AGREEMENT FOR SALE made at _____ on this _____ day of _____ in the Christian Year Two Thousand _____ BETWEEN

M/s Shiv Parvati & Associates, a partnership firm having its office at _____, hereinafter called **"THE SELLER"** (which expression shall unless repugnant to the context or meaning thereof mean and include the partners or partner for the time being of the firm, the survivors or survivor of them and the heirs, executors and administrators of the last surviving partner and their/his/her assigns) of the One Part;

AND Reliant Industries Pvt. Ltd., a Company incorporated under the Indian Companies Act, 1956 having its Registered Office at _____, hereinafter called **"THE PURCHASERS"** (which expression shall unless repugnant to the context or meaning thereof be deemed to include its successors) of the Other Part;

WHEREAS the Seller is seized and possessed of and otherwise well and sufficiently entitled to all that piece and parcel of land hereditaments and property situate at _____, admeasuring approx. _____ sq. mtrs and described in the **Schedule** hereunder written (hereinafter called "**the said property**");

AND WHEREAS the Seller has agreed to sell and the Purchasers have agreed to purchase the said property at or for the price of Rs. _____ (Rupees _____ only) upon the terms and subject to the conditions hereinafter appearing.

NOW THIS AGREEMENT WITNESSETH AND IT IS HEREBY AGREED BY AND BETWEEN THE PARTIES HERETO as follows:

1. The Seller shall sell and the Purchasers shall purchase all and singular

the said land hereditaments and property situate at _____ and delineated on the plan thereof hereto annexed being thereon shown surrounded by red coloured boundary line and more particularly described in the Schedule hereunder written with their appurtenances, free from all encumbrances, at or for the price of Rs. _____/- (Rupees _____ only).

2. The aforesaid consideration shall be paid by the Purchasers to the Seller as the price of the said property in the manner following that is to say:–

   (a) Rs. _____/- (Rupees _____ only) as deposit or earnest money shall be paid on or before the execution of these presents (the payment and receipt whereof the Seller doth hereby admit and acknowledge); and

   (b) Rs. _____/- (Rupees _____ only) the balance of the sale price shall be paid within _____ from the date hereof on completion of the sale as hereinafter provided.

3. In case the Purchaser willfully delays payment of the aforesaid consideration, the Seller shall be entitled to charge the Purchaser interest of ____% p.a. for the period of the delay.

4. The Seller shall deliver the title deeds relating to the said property in his possession or power within _____ days from the date hereof for inspection hereof by the Purchaser or his Advocate for investigation of title. The said documents may be handed over to the Purchaser's Advocate against his personal acknowledgement/accountable receipt for the sake of convenience, if so required by the Purchaser's Advocate.

5. The Seller shall make out a marketable title to the said property free from all encumbrances, doubts and claims and shall at his own costs and expenses get in all outstanding estates and clear all defects in the title encumbrances and claims by way of sale exchange, mortgage, gift, trust, inheritance, possession lease, lien, easement or otherwise.

6. The sale will be completed within a period of _____ from the date hereof time being the essence of contract, in the following manner:

   (a) _____ On payment of the balance consideration amount by the said Purchaser, as provided above, the Seller shall handover vacant and peaceful possession of the said property to the Purchasers;

   (b) The Seller shall deliver to the Purchasers all title deeds, documents and papers exclusively relating to the said property in his possession;

   (c) The Seller shall execute and deliver to the Purchasers or their nominee or nominees such Conveyance document or documents or assurances as may be required for effectuating a proper transfer of the said property to the names of the Purchasers or their nominees; and

   (d) The Seller shall execute a suitable and General Power of Attorney in favour of the Purchasers and/or their nominees to deal with the said property as full owners thereof including appointing Architects, preparing and submitting building and other plans for development of the said property making representations to and appearing before various authorities to make, sign, deliver and carry on correspondence, applications, writings, undertakings, affidavits and to negotiate with the existing tenants etc. The said Power of Attorney will be valid for a period of _____.

7. The Seller hereby declares and confirms as under:–

   (a) The Seller is otherwise well and sufficiently entitled to the said property described in the Schedule hereunder written. His title to the said property is free and marketable.

   (b) No other person except the Seller has any right, claim, interest or demand in respect of the said property or any part thereof.

   (c) The Seller has not created any sale, gift, mortgage, charge, lien, lease or any other adverse right or any other encumbrance whatsoever or howsoever on the said property and the said property is not subject to any claim or demand, encumbrance, attachment or any process issued by any Court or Authority and the Seller hereby declares that he shall hereafter not create any third party rights of whatsoever nature in respect of the said property.

(d) The Seller has not entered into any agreement or arrangement, oral or written with regard to the sale of the said property with any third party;

(e) There are no proceedings instituted by or against the Seller in respect of the said property and pending in any Court or before any authority; and

(f) The said property is his self acquired property.

8. The Seller further declares that no notices including any notice for acquisition, requisition or set back by the Government Central or State or by the Municipal Corporation or any other local, or public body or authority in respect of the said property have been issued to, served upon or received by the Seller or his agent or any person on his behalf and that all previous notices and requisitions have been duly complied with by the Seller. If any such notices other than a notice for acquisition, requisition or set-back is hereafter issued to, served upon or received by the Seller or any person on his behalf in respect of the said property before the completion of the sale herein, the Seller shall forthwith give notice thereof to the Purchasers and shall comply with the same at his own costs and expenses.

9. If before the completion of the sale herein any notice for requisition or set-back is issued to, received by or served upon the Seller, it shall be at the option of the Purchasers to terminate this Agreement and upon such termination of this Agreement the Seller shall forthwith return to the Purchasers the earnest money but without interest and each party

shall bear and pay all costs of and incidental to the sale incurred by them upto the date of such determination.

10. If the Seller shall have willfully concealed any notice issued, served or received as aforesaid the Purchasers will be entitled to all costs charges and expenses of and incidental to the Agreement for sale incurred by them upto the date of such determination.

11. If any notice is issued, published served by Government or any local or public authority for acquisition of the said property or any part thereof (for any party other than the Purchasers) this Agreement shall at the option of the Purchasers to be exercised within 30 days of the knowledge of such notice be null and void and the Seller shall thereupon forthwith return to the Purchasers the earnest money and all other moneys received hereunder but without interest and each party will bear and pay their own costs charges and expenses.

12. In the event of the sale not being completed due to any willful default on the part of the Seller, the Purchasers shall have the right to require specific performance by the Seller of this Agreement.

13. In the event of the sale not being completed due to any willful default on the part of the Purchasers, the Seller shall have the right to require specific performance by the Purchasers of this Agreement or alternatively to forfeit the earnest money and to require the Purchasers to pay to the Seller the costs incurred by the Seller..

14. The Seller shall pay all assessments, rents, rates, taxes and out goings in respect of the said property previous to the day of handing over possession and the completion of the sale.

15. The stamp-duty, registration charges and all other out of pocket expenses payable on this deed shall be borne by _____. However, each party shall bear and pay their own Advocates professional fees.

IN WITNESS WHEREOF the parties hereto have executed these presents and a duplicate hereof the day and year first hereinabove written.

THE SCHEDULE ABOVE REFERRED TO:

ALL THAT plot of land together with _____ thereon bearing No. _____, admeasuring approx. _____ sq. mtrs situate at _____ in the village _____, Taluka _____, in the Registration Sub-district of _____, District.

SIGNED AND DELIVERED BY THE	)
Withinnamed SELLER,	)
M/s Shiv Parvati & Associates	)
by the hand of its partner	)
_____,	)
in the presence of	)
1.	)
2.	)
THE COMMON SEAL OF the withinnamed	)
PURCHASERS, **Reliant Industries Pvt. Ltd.,**	)
is hereunto affixed pursuant to the	)
Resolution of its Board of Directors	)
passed in that behalf, on the	)
day of _____ 200___ in the presence of	)
(1) _____, Managing Director	)
and (2) _____, Director	)
in the presence of	)
1.	)
2.	)

2
Mortgage

A Mortgage is the transfer of an interest in specific immovable property for purpose of securing the payment of money advanced by way of loan and also as an existing or future debt.

The transferor is *the mortgagor* and the transferee, *the mortgagee*. The instrument which is executed between the mortgagor and the mortgagee is the *mortgage deed*. The money which is advanced is called the *mortgage money*.

■ Example : Raj has availed of a loan of Rs. 10,00,000/- from Bank of India against mortgage of his flat, No.10 in Kusum Co-operative Housing Society Ltd. and had executed a deed of mortgage with the bank. Raj has transferred his interest as owner of his flat in Kusum Co-operative Housing Society Ltd. to Bank of India for the purpose of obtaining Rs.10,00,000/- i.e. the mortgage money.

Essential Elements
- There should be transfer of an interest in specific immovable property.
- Transfer of an interest must be for securing the payment of money.
- The money can be advanced by way of loan and as an existing or future debt.

TYPES OF MORTGAGES

A. Simple Mortgage

In a simple mortgage, there is no release of possession of the mortgaged property in favour of the mortgagee. Upon failure by the mortgagor to repay the mortgage money, the mortgagee has a right to sell the mortgaged property and apply the proceeds of the sale for re-payment of the mortgage money.

B. Mortgage by Conditional Sale

In a conditional sale, the mortgagor 'ostensibly sells' (appears to sell) the mortgaged property to the mortgagee on condition that if the mortgagor fails to pay the mortgage money, the sale becomes complete *or* if the mortgagor repays the mortgage money then the sale becomes null and void. On repayment of the mortgage money, the mortgagee shall transfer the property to the Mortgagor.

C. Usufructuary Mortgage

In a usufructuary mortage, the mortgagor delivers possession of the property to the mortgagee. He authorizes the mortgagee to retain possession of the property till repayment of the mortgage money. The mortgagee is entitled to receive the profits and rents of the property and appropriate the same in payment of the mortgage money.

■ Example: A mortgaged his property to B and asked his tenants to pay the rent to B. In this case, B is entitled to receive the rent and appropriate the same towards repayment of his loan.

D. English Mortgage

In an English mortgage, the mortgagor binds himself for repayment of the mortgage money on a certain date, on the condition that the mortgagee will retransfer the mortgaged property to him, which is in the possession of the mortgagee.

E. Deposit of Title deeds

Any person from Mumbai, Kolkata and Chennai or any other place specified by the State Government can deliver documents of title of an immovable property to a creditor, as a security for securing the payment of the mortgage money. It is also called Equitable Mortgage. No agreement is necessary for this mortgage. A simple letter showing intention of creating a mortgage by deposit of title deeds is sufficient to prove the creation of such mortgage.

F. Anomalous Mortgage

Any other mortgage (other than the ones discussed) is known as an Anomalous Mortgage.

RIGHTS AND LIABILITIES OF THE MORTGAGOR

On payment of the mortgage money, the Mortgagor is entitled to:

(1) delivery of the mortgage deeds and all documents relating to the mortgaged property which are in possession of the mortgagee.
(2) delivery of the mortgaged property which is in possession of the mortgagee.
(3) re-transfer of the mortgaged property to him or any other person, as he directs, at his own cost.
(4) inspect the documents relating to the mortgaged property which is in the custody of the mortgagee.
(5) any improvements made to the mortgaged property. However, if such improvement made by the mortgagee was necessary to preserve the property or save the property from destruction or deterioration, the mortgagor is bound to pay proper cost incurred by the mortgagee in addition to the principal money.

■ Example : Rajnath mortgaged his plot of agriculture land to Raghav. To protect the crops from animals, Raghav installed an electric fence covering the whole plot at his own cost. Rajnath is bound to pay Raghav for the additional expenses incurred on fencing the plot.

RIGHTS AND LIABILITIES OF THE MORTGAGEE

(1) When the mortgage money is due, the mortgagee has a right to obtain an order from the court to :
    (i) prohibit the mortgagor from exercising his right to redeem the property.
    (ii) to cause the property to be sold. This is known as *Suit for foreclosure*.
(2) The mortgagee has a right to sue for the mortgage money:

(i) where the mortgagor binds himself to repay the same and has failed to pay.

(ii) where the mortgaged property is wholly or partly destroyed, or the security is rendered insufficient, or when, despite reasonable opportunitunities given by the mortgagee, the mortgagor fails to rectify the deficiency.

3. the mortgagee must manage the mortgaged property which is in his custody and must take care of it as if it were his own.

SAMPLE

DEED OF MORTGAGE

THIS DEED OF MORTGAGE executed at _____ this _____ day of _____ 200__ between

M/s. Lokhande Associates a partnership firm having its office at _____, hereinafter called **"THE MORTGAGOR"** (which expression shall unless repugnant to the context or meaning thereof mean and include the partners or partner for the time being of the firm, the survivors or survivor of them and the heirs, executors and administrators of the last surviving partner and their/his/her assigns) of the ONE PART;

AND

Indian Funding Company Pvt. Ltd., a Company incorporated under the Indian Companies Act, 1956 having its Registered Office at _____, hereinafter called **"THE MORTGAGEE"** (which expression shall unless repugnant to the context or meaning thereof be deemed to include its successors) of the OTHER PART;

WHEREAS:

(a) The Mortgagor is the Owner of and well and sufficiently seized and possessed of the property more particularly described in the Schedule hereunder written (hereinafter referred to as "**the said property**").

(b) The Mortgagor is in need of money for paying certain business debts and liabilities and has approached the Mortgagee to advance them a loan of Rs. 2,00,00,000/- (Rupees Two Crores only).

(c) Pursuant to the said request of the Mortgagor, the Mortgagee agreed to lend and advance to the Mortgagor a sum of **Rs.** _____ against the security of the said property by way of mortgage for securing repayment of the principal and interest thereof in the manner hereinafter appearing.

NOW THIS INDENTURE WITNESSETH that in pursuance of the said agreement and in consideration of the sum of Rs. _____ paid to the Mortgagor by the Mortgagee on or before execution hereof (the receipt whereof the Mortgagor doth hereby admit and acknowledge and of and from the same doth hereby release and discharge the Mortgagee) the Mortgagor doth hereby covenant with the Mortgagee that the Mortgagor shall pay to the Mortgagee the said sum of Rs. _____ together with interest thereof from the date hereof at the agreed rate of 5 (five) percent per month with monthly rests by equal monthly installments.

The first of such payments shall be made on the _____ day of _____ and the subsequent payments shall be made on or before 5th day of each and every following month, the last of such monthly installment of the principal amount together with all accrued installments and interest thereof being payable on the _____ day of _____ (hereinafter called "**the due date**") and will also pay after the due date so long as the said sum of Rs. _____ or any part thereof or interest thereof shall remain unpaid to the Mortgagee in the manner aforesaid.

If any payment of interest is not made on the respective due dates of the installments it shall be added to the principal sum and compounded every month accordingly and shall be chargeable upon the mortgaged property for all intents and purposes recorded herein, however, this provision shall not in any way permit the Mortgagor to allow any interest or the monthly agreed installment towards the principal amount to fall in arrears nor shall it in anywise interfere with, prejudice, limit or affect the right of sale or any other powers or remedies for securing and enforcing payment of the Mortgage debt hereunder payable.

AND PROVIDED FURTHER THAT NOTWITHSTANDING the covenant to repay the principal amount in agreed monthly installments and in the event of the Mortgagor committing default in payment of any two of such monthly installments, in that event the due date for repayment of the entire principal amount together with all accrued interest shall stand accelerated to the date of the last of such second default entitling the Mortgagee to at once demand the said entire mortgage debt.

PROVIDED always that if the Mortgagor shall pay to the Mortgagee the said sum of Rs. _____ on the _____ day of _____ 200____ together with the agreed rate of interest and in the aforestated manner and also all other moneys by law or under these presents payable by the Mortgagor to the Mortgagee (hereinafter collectively referred to as "**the Mortgage amount**") then and in such case the Mortgagee shall at the request, cost, charges and expenses of the Mortgagor release the said property by executing the Deed of Reconveyance.

THE SCHEDULE ABOVE REFERRED TO:

(Description of the said property)

IN WITNESS WHEREOF the parties hereto have executed these presents the day and year first hereinabove written.

SIGNED AND DELIVERED BY THE	)
Withinnamed MORTGAGOR,	)
M/s. Lokhande Associates,	)
by the hand of its partner	)
_____,	)

in the presence of	)
1.	)
2.	)
THE COMMON SEAL OF the withinnamed	)
MORTGAGEES, **Indian Funding Pvt. Ltd.**,	)
is hereunto affixed pursuant to the	)
Resolution of its Board of Directors	)
passed in that behalf, on the _____	)
day of _____ 200____ in the presence of	)
(1) _____, Managing Director	)
and (2) _____, Director	)

3
Lease

A lease of immovable property is a transfer of a right to enjoy the property. It is made for a certain period of time, express or implied, or in perpetuity. The consideration is the price paid or promised to be paid, a share of crops, service or any other thing of value. The consideration can be given periodically or on specified occasions, to the transferor by the transferee.

The transferor is called the *lessor*. The transferee is called the *lessee*. The price is called the *premium* and the money, a share of crops, service or any other thing to be given is called *rent*.

■ Example : MHADA (Maharashtra Housing and Area Development Authority) granted a lease of Plot No.102 to Shakuntala Co-operative Society Ltd., for 30 years for a rent amount of Rs.1000 per month. In this case, MHADA (Lessor) is transferring the right to enjoy the property i.e. Plot no.102 to the Society (the lessee) for 30 years. The rent is Rs.1000 per month.

RIGHTS AND LIABILITIES OF THE LESSOR

(1) The lessor is bound to make known to the lessee, any material defect in the property with reference to its proposed use, of which he is aware.

(2) The lessor must put the lessee in possession of the property.

(3) The lessor must make sure that the lessee should hold the property without any interruption.

Lease

RIGHTS AND LIABILITIES OF THE LESSEE

(1) If the property given on lease is destroyed by natural calamities or rendered unfit for the proposed use, the lessee can terminate the lease agreement.

(2) If the lessor neglects to repair the property or fails to make any payment related to the property which he is bound to make, within reasonable time, the lessee can carry out the repairs or make the payment at his own cost, and deduct the same from the rent payable to the lessor.

(3) The lessee is bound to take care of the property leased to him and restore the same in as good a condition as it was at the time when he received possession.

(4) The lessee must bring to the notice of the lessor, any proceedings or encroachment on the property leased to him.

(5) The lessee may use the property and its products (if any) with proper care and must not use or allow another to use the property for a purpose other than that for which it was given. He also, should not carry out any work which will be destructive or will cause permanent damage to the property. For example mining work etc.

(6) The lessee is bound to pay the premium or rent to the lessor or his agent.

(7) On termination of the lease, the lessee is bound to hand over the possession of the property to the lessor.

DETERMINATION OF LEASE

A lease of immovable property terminates by :

* *Conditional time limit,* based on the occurence of some future event - and the event happens.

* *Express or implied surrender* : of the lease, by the lessee.

* *Forfeiture* - where the lessee breaks any condition on which the lessor has the right to re-enter into the property.

* *Expiration of a notice to terminate the lease :* On a notice given by the lessor to the lessee, the lease property is handed over to the lessor.

LEASE

THIS INDENTURE made at _____ on this _____ day of _____ two thousand _____, BETWEEN

M/s Prithvi Development Corporation a partnership firm having its office at _____, hereinafter called "**THE LESSOR**" (which expression shall unless repugnant to the context or meaning thereof mean and include the partners or partner for the time being of the firm, the survivors or survivor of them and the heirs, executors and administrators of the last surviving partner and their/his/her assigns) of the One Part;

AND Mr. Altaf Khan, sole proprietor of Khan Developers, having its office at _____, hereinafter called "**The LESSEE**" (which expression shall unless it be repugnant to the context or meaning thereof be deemed to mean and include his heirs, executors, and administrators) of the Other Part;

WHEREAS:

(a) The Lessor vide an Agreement for Sale dated _____ had purchased _____ (hereinafter referred to as "the Office") from Mumbai Developers Pvt. Ltd., hereinafter referred to as the Developers.

(b) The Lessor has agreed to demise to the Lessee the said Office for the period of 10 years and at the rent and upon the terms and conditions recorded herein.

(c) At the request of the Lessee, the Lessor has agreed to execute these presents in favour of the Lessee.

NOW THIS INDENTURE WITNESSETH AS FOLLOWS:

1. In consideration of the rent and Lessee's covenants hereinafter reserved and contained the Lessor doth hereby demise Unto the Lessee the said Office TO HOLD UNTO the Lessee the premises hereby demised (here-

after for brevity's sake referred to as "**the demised premises**") from the _____ day of _____ Two thousand ___ for the term of 10 years (ten years) yielding and paying the yearly rent of Rs. _____ (Rupees _____ only), and which rent shall be payable by the Lessee to the Lessor on or before 10th day of ____ every year in advance.

2. The Lessee doth hereby expressly covenant with the Lessor as under:–

    (a) That he will during the said term regularly pay to the Lessor the aforesaid yearly rent without deduction and in all the circumstances in the manner aforesaid. In the event of any delay, the Lessee shall pay interest on the arrears at the rate of _____ per cent per annum from the due date till payment.

    (b) That he will also pay and discharge all rates, taxes charges, duties, burdens, assessments, outgoings and impositions whatsoever now payable or hereafter during the said term to become payable and now or hereafter during the said term assessed charged or imposed upon the demised premises or any part thereof.

    (c) That he will in executing the works aforesaid and at all times during the continuance of this demise observe and conform to all such rules and regulations of the Municipal Corporation of ____ and other authorities as may be in force for the time being relating to buildings.

    (d) That he will not do or cause or suffer to be done upon the Office any act which shall be a nuisance or annoyance, or be injurious or offensive to the owners of any neighboring premises.

    (e) That he will indemnify and keep indemnified the Lessor against all suits, claims and demands in respect of the demised premises.

    (f) That he will at the expiration or sooner determination of the said term quietly surrender and deliver up to the Lessor the said Office in such good and substantial repair and condition and so maintained, saved and cleansed and in all respects in such state and condition as shall be consistent with the due performance of the several covenants hereinbefore contained.

(g) The Lessee shall not assign transfer or part with the possession of the Office or any part thereof to any person without previously obtaining the written consent of the Lessor which consent shall not be unreasonably withheld.

3. PROVIDED ALWAYS AND IT IS AGREED and declared that if the rent hereby reserved or any part thereof shall be in arrears, for thirty days after the same shall have become due and whenever there shall be a breach or non-performance or non-observance by the Lessee of any of the Covenants, conditions or agreements herein contained, it shall be lawful for the Lessor to re-enter upon the Office or any part thereof in the name of the whole and immediately thereupon this demise and all rights of the Lessee hereunder shall stand absolutely determined but without prejudice to any right or remedy of the Lessor already accrued and then subsisting PROVIDED HOWEVER before making such re-entry in respect of any breach of covenant, notice in writing shall have been given to the Lessee intimating the breach of covenant. If the Lessee fails to make good such breach within _____ months of the date of service of such notice, the Lessor shall be entitled to re-enter upon the Office or any part thereof and thereafter the Lease shall stand determined provided always that such re-entry shall be without prejudice to any right of action or remedy of the Lessor in respect of any antecedent breach of any of the covenants on the part of the Lessee. The term for payment of interest on the arrears of rent shall not prejudice or affect the right of re-entry herein contained.

4. He the Lessor doth hereby covenant with the Lessee that the lessee paying the rent hereinabove reserved and performing and observing all the covenants, conditions and agreements on the part of the Lessee hereinbefore contained shall peaceably hold and enjoy the demised premises during the said term without any interruption by the Lessor or any person claiming under him.

IN WITNESS WHEREOF the parties have hereunto set and subscribed their respective hands, the day and year first hereinabove written.

THE SCHEDULE ABOVE REFERRED TO:

(Give description of the premises)

SIGNED AND DELIVERED by the	)
withinnamed Lessor,	)
M/s Prithvi Development Corporation	)
by the hand of its partner/s	)
_____,	)
in the presence of	)
1.	)
2.	)
SIGNED AND DELIVERED by the	)
withinnamed Lessee, Mr. Altaf Khan,	)
sole proprietor of Khan Developers,	)
in the presence of	)
1.	)
2.	)

4
Exchange

WHAT IS AN EXCHANGE?

An exchange takes place when two persons mutually transfer the ownership of one thing for the ownership of another. Neither or both things should be only money. Such a transaction is called an Exchange.

The definition of exchange is not limited only to immovable property. It also includes movable property.

Essential elements of an exchange are:

- two parties.
- parties should *mutually agree* to transfer the ownership of property.
- neither or both things should be only money. If the consideration is money, it becomes a sale.
- however, money may form part of the consideration.

■ Example : Raj transferred his flat which was valued at Rs.15,00,000/- to Shyam, and Shyam transferred his farm house, worth Rs.15,00,000/- to Raj. This transaction is an exchange. Here, Raj is transferring the ownership of his flat in exchange for the ownership of the farm house.

If the value of Raj's flat is say Rs. 25,00,000/- and he intends to exchange his flat with Shyam's farm house worth Rs.15,00,000, then Shyam will pay the difference of Rs. 10 lakh, in money.

Exchange

MODE OF TRANSFER

The exchange of immovable property above Rs.100/- if not made by a registered instrument, is invalid.

In an exchange it is not necessary that there should be two separate deeds.

RIGHTS OF A PARTY WHO SUFFERS A LOSS

A party to the exchange is said to have suffered loss when he is deprived of the thing or any part of the thing exchanged, due to a defect in the title of the other party. The aggrieved person is entitled to have the thing which he had transferred to the other party, returned, though it is in custody of the other party.

In the above example, Raj transferred his flat to Shyam in exchange of a farm house. Later, Raj discovered that Shyam is not the owner of the house. Raj is entitled to his flat being returned by Shyam, which is in his (Shyam's) possession.

RIGHTS AND LIABILITIES OF PARTIES

Under an exchange, each party has the rights and liabilities of a *seller*, regarding what he gives, and the rights and liabilities of a *buyer*, with regard to what he receives.

However, an exchange does not involve the payment of money and therefore there cannot be a claim on property for 'unpaid price'. Also, when money is paid for the equality of an exchange, there is no charge for the money so paid.

■ Example : Raj transferred his flat of Rs.15,00,000/- to Shyam and Shyam transferred his farm house worth Rs.14,00,000/- and paid Rs.1,00,000/- in cash to Raj. If Shyam fails to pay Rs.1,00,000/-, Raj cannot have a charge on the farm house for Rs.1,00,000/-.

DIFFERENCE BETWEEN SALE AND EXCHANGE

In a *sale*, there is exchange of a thing, for a price. In an *exchange*, the transfer of ownership of a thing is always for the transfer of ownership of a thing in return.

DEED OF EXCHANGE

THIS INDENTURE made at _____ on this _____ day of _____ two thousand _____, BETWEEN

Mr. R. R. Shinde of _____, Indian Inhabitant, hereinafter called "**the Party of the One Part**": (which expression shall unless it be repugnant to the context or meaning thereof mean and include his heirs, executors and administrators) of the One Part:

AND Mr. A. D. Kothari of _____, Indian Inhabitant, hereinafter called "**the Party of the Second Part**" (which expression shall unless it be repugnant to the context or meaning thereof mean and include his heirs, executors and administrators) of the Other Part:

WHEREAS the party of the One Part is seized and possessed of or otherwise well and sufficiently entitled free from encumbrances to _____ _____ (1st Flat), and more particularly described in the **First Schedule** hereunder written;

AND WHEREAS the party of the Second Part is seized and possessed of or otherwise well and sufficiently entitled free from encumbrances to _____ _____ (2nd Flat), and more particularly described in the **Second Schedule** hereunder written;

AND WHEREAS the Parties hereto propose to exchange the said two Flats among themselves as it is advantageous to both of them.

AND WHEREAS they have now entered into this Deed.

1. The party of the One Part is seized and possessed of or otherwise well and sufficiently entitled free from encumbrances to _____ _____ (1st Flat), and more particularly described in the **First Schedule** hereunder written.

2. The party of the Second Part is seized and possessed of or otherwise well and sufficiently entitled free from encumbrances to _____ _____ (2nd Flat), and more particularly described in the **Second Schedule** hereunder written.

3. The value the 1ˢᵗ Flat is Rs. _____/- and the value of the 2ⁿᵈ Flat, is Rs. _____/-.
4. The party of the one part hereby transfers the ownership of property being 1st Flat to the party fo the 2nd part AND the party of 2nd part transfers the ownership of property being 2nd flat to the party of the one part.
5. Since the difference in the value of both the Flats, i.e. 1ˢᵗ Flat and 2ⁿᵈ Flat, is Rs. _____/- (the "said difference"), the Party of the Second Part shall pay the Party of the First Part the said difference within _____ of the execution of this Deed.
6. On any willful default on the Party of the Second Part in paying the said consideration, the Party of the First Part shall be entitled to charge the Party of the Second Part interest of ___% p.a. for the period of delay.
7. The stamp duty and registration charges in respect of the present instrument shall be shared equally between the parties hereto.

IN WITNESS WHEREOF the parties hereto have hereunto set and subscribed their respective hands the day and year first hereinabove written.

First schedule above referred to:

(1ˢᵗ Flat)

SECOND SCHEDULE ABOVE REFERRED TO:

(2ⁿᵈ Flat)

SIGNED AND DELIVERED by)
the withinnamed **Mr. R. R. Shinde**)
in the presence of:)
1.)
2.)
SIGNED AND DELIVERED by the)
withinnamed **Mr. A. D. Kothari**)
in the presence of:)
1.)
2.)

5
Gift

A Gift is the transfer of certain existing movable or immovable property, made voluntarily and without consideration.

PARTIES TO THE GIFT

A gift is made by a person, the *donor* to another, the *donee*, and accepted by or on behalf of the donee.

A gift should be made out of one's own free will. It is always without consideration i.e. without payment of money.

■ Example: Ajay gifted his flat, No.10 in ABC Co-operative Housing Society Limited, to his son Vijay. In this case, Ajay (Donor) transferred his flat to his son Vijay (Donee) out of natural love and affection, by way of a gift. To complete the transaction of a gift, the above flat should be accepted by Vijay during the lifetime of the donor.

ESSENTIAL ELEMENTS OF A GIFT

- There should be two parties, the donor and donee.
- There must be a transfer of *certain* existing movable or immovable property.
- It should be made by voluntarily by the donor i.e. of his own accord.
- There must be absence of consideration (money).
- It should be accepted by the donee during the lifetime of the donor.

Gift

TRANSFER OF PROPERTY AS A GIFT

A gift of *immovable property* must be made by a registered instrument, signed by, or on behalf of the donor and attested by at least two witnesses.

A gift of *movable property* may be made either by registered instrument, signed as aforesaid or by delivery of the property.

SUSPENSION OR REVOCATION OF A GIFT

The donor or donee may agree that on the possible occurence of a specified event, which does not depend on will of the donor, the gift shall be suspended or revoked.

In the above example, Ajay gifted his flat to his son Vijay, on condition that if Vijay dies before him, he can take back the flat. In this eventuality, the gift stands revoked.

However, a gift which is revocable wholly, or in part, at the mere will of the donor, is invalid, wholly, or in part, as the case may be.

In the above case, Ajay gifted his flat and Rs.10,000 to his son Vijay, reserving the right to take back Rs.10,000/- as and when he needs it. The gift holds good as far as the flat is concerned but is invalid with regards to the Rs.10,000/-.

ONEROUS GIFTS

When a gift is in the form of a single transfer to the same person of several things, of which one is and others are not burdened by an obligation, the donee can take nothing, unless he accepts it fully. Thus he can either accept it fully or reject it fully.

■ Example : Ritesh is the owner of Plot A. The area of the plot is 950 sq ft., of which 500 sq. ft is mortgaged with Bank of India. Ritesh gifted plot A to his nephew Rakesh. Rakesh can either accept the Plot A burdened with the mortgage or he can reject it wholly. He cannot accept only 450 sq ft. and reject the 500 sq.ft which is mortgaged with the bank.

When a gift is in the form of two or more separate and independent transfers to the same person for several things, the donee is at liberty to accept one of them and refuse the other, although the former is beneficial and the latter, burdensome.

■ Example: Ritesh is the owner of plot A, plot B and plot C. Plot A is mortgaged with Bank of India. Ritesh gifted all three plots to his nephew Rakesh through separate gift deeds. Rakesh has the liberty to accept plot B and C and reject Plot A which is mortgaged with the bank.

A gift comprising both, existing and future property is invalid as far as the future property is concerned.

SPECIMEN

DEED OF GIFT

THIS DEED OF GIFT executed at _____, this day of _____ Two thousand and _____ BETWEEN

Mr. D. D. Kapoor of _____, Indian Inhabitant, residing at _____, hereinafter called "THE DONOR" (which expression shall unless it be repugnant to the context or meaning thereof mean and include his heirs, executors and administrators) of the One Part;

AND Mrs P. K. Khanna of _____, Indian Inhabitant, residing at _____, hereinafter called "THE DONEE" (which expression shall unless it be repugnant to the context or meaning thereof, mean and include his heirs, executors, administrators and assigns) of the Other Part:

WHEREAS:

(a) The Donor is absolutely seized and possessed of or otherwise well and sufficiently entitled to the plot of land bearing No. _____, admeasuring approx. _____ sq.mts. situate at _____ _____ together with structures standing thereon and more particularly described in the **Schedule** hereunder written and delineated on the plan thereof hereto annexed and shown with red colour boundary line thereon and hereafter referred to as **"the said property"**.

(b) The DONEE is the married daughter of the DONOR.

Gift

(c) The Donor intends to gift the said property to the Donee in consideration of natural love and affection which the DONOR bears towards the DONEE.

(d) The DONEE has accepted the said gift by executing these presents;

NOW THIS INDENTURE WITNESSETH that for effectuating his said desire and in consideration of natural love and affection which the Donor bears towards the Donee, the Donor doth hereby grant, convey, transfer and assure unto the Donee **ALL THAT** piece or parcel of land or ground with the messuages hereditaments and premises situate at _____ admeasuring approx _____ sq.mts and more particularly described in the **Schedule** hereunder written and delineated on the plan thereof hereto annexed and thereon shown surrounded by red coloured boundary line.

TOGETHER WITH all and singular the structures, houses, outhouses, fencing, compound walls, edifices, buildings, court yards, areas, compounds, sewers drains ditches fences trees plants, shrubs ways paths passages commons gullies wells waters water-courses lights liberties privileges easements profits advantages rights members and appurtenances whatsoever to the said land or ground hereditaments and premises or any part thereof belonging or in any wise appurtenant to or with the same or any part thereof now or at or any time hereto before usually held used occupied or enjoyed or reputed or known as part or member thereof and to belong or be appurtenant thereto.

AND ALL THE ESTATE right, title, interest, claim and demand whatsoever at law and in equity of the Donor in to out of or upon the said land hereditaments and premises or any part thereof.

TO HAVE AND TO HOLD all and singular the said hereditaments and premises hereby granted conveyed, transferred and assured or intended or expressed so to be with their and every of their rights members and appurtenances (all which are hereinafter called "**the said property**") **UNTO AND TO THE USE** and benefit of the Donee, his heirs, executors, Administrators and assigns for ever.

SUBJECT TO the payment of all future rates assessments taxes and dues now chargeable upon the same or hereafter to become payable to the Government or to the Municipal Corporation or any other public body or local authority in respect thereof.

AND the Donor doth hereby for himself and his heirs, executors and administrators covenant with the Donee **THAT** notwithstanding any act, deed, matter or thing whatsoever by the Donor or any person or persons lawfully or equitably claiming by from through under or in trust for them made done committed omitted or knowingly or willingly suffered to the contrary, the Donor now hath in himself good right full power and absolute authority to grant convey transfer and assure the said premises hereby granted conveyed transferred and assured or intended so to be unto and to the use of the Donee in manner aforesaid.

AND THAT it shall be lawful for the Donee from time to time and at all times hereafter peaceably and quietly to hold enter upon use occupy possess and enjoy the said premises hereby granted conveyed transferred and assured with their appurtenances and receive the rents issues and profits thereof and of every part thereof to and for his own use and benefit without any suit or lawful eviction, interruption, claim and demand whatsoever from or by the Donor or his heirs, executors and administrators or its successors and Assigns or any of them from or by any person lawfully or equitably claiming or to claim by from under or in trust for them.

AND THAT free and clear and freely and clearly and absolutely acquitted exonerated released and for ever discharged or otherwise by the Donor well and sufficiently saved defended kept harmless and indemnified of from and against all former and other estates title charges and encumbrances whatsoever had made executed occasioned or suffered by the Donor or by any other person or persons lawfully or equitably claiming or to claim by from under or in trust for them.

AND FURTHER that he the Donor and all persons having or lawfully or equitably claiming any estate, right, title or interest at law or in equity in the said premises hereby granted conveyed transferred and assured or any part thereof by from under or in trust for them the Donor shall and will from time to time and at all times hereafter at the request and cost of the Donee do and execute or cause to be done and executed all such further and other lawful and reasonable acts, deeds, matters and things conveyances and assurances in law whatsoever for the better further and more perfectly and absolutely granting unto and to the use of the Donee in manner aforesaid as shall or may be reasonably required by the Donee his heirs, executors, Administrators or assigns or their Counsel in law for assuring the said premises and every part thereof hereby granted conveyed transferred and assured unto and to the use of the Donee in manner aforesaid.

AND the Donor doth hereby confirm and record that he has on execution hereof put the Donee in quiet, peaceful and vacant possession of the said property as owners thereof.

THE SCHEDULE ABOVE REFERRED TO:

ALL THAT plot of land together with structures thereon bearing No. _____, admeasuring approx. _____ sq.mtrs situate at _____ _____ in the _____, _____, in the Registration Sub-district of _____, District.

IN WITNESS WHEREOF the DONOR as well as the DONEE by way of acceptance of the said gift, have put their respective hands on the day and year first hereinabove written.

SIGNED AND DELIVERED by)
the withinnamed Mr. D. D. Kapoor,)
the DONOR abovenamed, in)
the presence of ———————)
(1)
(2)
SIGNED, AND DELIVERED by)
the withinnamed Mrs P. K. Khanna,)
the DONEE abovenamed,)
in the presence of ———————)
(1)
(2)

6

Lis Pendens

Under the doctrine of Lis Pendens, transfer of any immovable property during the pendency of the suit relating to the immoveable property is prohibited.

Let us discuss this principle in detail.

If a suit or proceeding is pending in any court, in which suit or proceeding any right of the immovable property is in question, then the parties to the suit or proceeding cannot deal with or transfer the immovable property. This is so that the rights of the other party to the property are not affected. The court's permission is required for such a dealing or transaction.

Points to be noted

- There should be a pendency of any suit or proceeding in a court.
- The court must have authority within the limits of India.
- The suit or proceeding must be in relation to any right of the immovable property in question.
- The parties to the suit or proceeding cannot deal with or transfer the immovable property without authority of the court.
- A suit or proceeding is said to continue till such date that it has been disposed off by a final decree or order of the court.

■ Example : Raj entered into an agreement with Rakesh to sell his flat no. 2, Ravikiran Building, for Rs. 10,00,000/-. Rakesh paid Rs.2,00,000/- and failed to pay the balance consideration. Raj filed a suit against Rakesh for the balance consideration. During the pendency of the suit, Raj sold the flat to Ritu.

The principle of lis pendens, prohibits the transfer of the immovable property during the pendancy of the suit and therefore, Raj cannot transfer his flat to Ritu. However, if the court passes a decree in favour of Rakesh, then the agreement between Raj and Ritu will stand void.

Under this principle, the pendency of a suit or proceeding, will commence from the date of the presentation of the plaint or the institution of the proceedings in a Court of competent jurisdiction i.e. the Court which has authority to decide the Suit.

A suit or proceeding will continue:

- till such date that it is disposed off by a final judgment or order of the court.
- till the complete satisfaction or discharge of such decree or order has been obtained.
- till it becomes impossible to implement the decree or order, due to the expiry of its period.

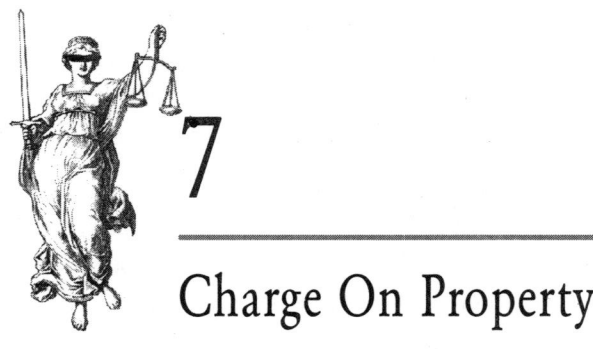

Charge On Property

Where immovable property of one person (A) is, by the act of parties or operation of law, made security for the payment of money to another (B) and where the transaction does not amount to a mortgage, the latter (i.e. B) is said to have a charge on the property.

CHARGE BY AN ACT OF PARTIES

A charge may be created by an act of parties. No particular form of words is necessary. The *intention* of the parties to make the property security for the payment of money is sufficient.

■ Example : Manisha acquired property according to the Will of her mother, Durgadevi. The Will also contains a provision stating, Rs.1000 per month from the said property should be given to Raju. Thus, Raju has a charge on the estate.

CHARGE BY OPERATION OF LAW

A Charge may be created by operation of law.

■ Example : Lalita obtained a consent decree passed in a Divorce petition she had filed against her husband Rajesh. Under one of the provisions of the decree, Rajesh should pay Rs.2000 to Lalita, from his residential property, as medical expenses. Thus, Lalita has a charge on the property.

DIFFERENCE BETWEEN CHARGE AND MORTAGE

- A charge is a security for the payment of money while a mortgage is a security for the payment of a debt.
- In a mortgage, there is transfer of an interest in specific immovable property. However, charge only gives a right to payment without transferring an interest, in specific immovable property.
- A mortgagee can recover money from any person who becomes entitled to the security. It is immaterial whether the person is aware of the mortgage or not. However, a charge can be enforced only against the transferee who has notice of the charge.
- A charge may be created by an act of parties or operation of law. However, a mortgage may be created only by an act of parties.

REGISTRATION

There is no specific mode of creating a charge and it need not to be registered. But for a written charge, registration is necessary, as in the case of non-testamentary instrument of the value of Rs.100, or upward.

CHARGE BY TRUSTEE

The trustee of a trust property is entitled to a charge on it. Such a charge must be for the exact expenses incurred by him in the administration of the trust. However, he cannot file a suit for the sale of trust property to recover such expenses. He can reimburse the same out of the income and profits of the trust estate.

8

Part Performance

The doctrine of part performance protects the rights of the intended transferee.

MEANING

Where any person contracts to transfer for consideration (i.e. for money), any immovable property by writing signed by him or on his behalf *and*

By such writing, the terms necessary to constitute the transfer can be determined *and,*

Where in part performance of the contract, the transferee has taken possession of the property or if he is already in possession, he continues in possession of the property *and,*

Has done some act as required under the contract *and,*

The transferee has performed and willing to perform his part of the contract *and*

Irrespective of the fact that the contract required to be registered, has not been registered or where there is an instrument of transfer that has not been completed in the manner prescribed by the law.

Then,

The transferor is disqualified from enforcing any right against the transferee in respect of the property of which the transferee has taken or continued in possession.

Part Performance

■ **Example**: Manish entered into an agreement with Rita to sell his flat, No.11 for Rs. 10,00,000/-. Rita paid. Rs.2,00,000/- as earnest money, took possession of the flat and started renovating it as per the contract. The balance payment was to be made within 45 days of the Agreement.

After a month, Manish refused to sell the flat and filed a suit against Rita to get back the possession of the flat, although Rita was willing to pay the balance consideration. The court passed the decree in favour of Rita and ordered Manish to perform his part of the contract i.e. to complete the sale transaction.

Under the principle of part performance, Manish was disqualified from enforcing any rights relating to the flat since Rita was willing to perform her part of contract i.e. payment of the balance consideration. Besides, she was in possession of the flat and had started renovation work. Here, a series of acts were done by Rita in performance of the contract like payment of earnest money, renovation work etc. Therefore, the doctrine of part performance comes into the picture and Rita is thereby protected.

ESSENTIALS OF PART PERFORMANCE

- A person has agreed to transfer for money, any immovable property, in writing, signed by him or on his behalf.
- Transferee has taken possession of the property or if he is already in possession, he continues in possession of the property.
- Transferee must have done some act in the progression of the transaction.
- The transferee has performed and willing to perform his part of the contract.
- The contract that must be registered, has not been registered *or* where the instrument of transfer, has not been completed in the manner given by the law.

The doctrine of part performance also protects the rights of the transferee who has paid the consideration i.e. money, and who has no notice of the contract between the parties or part performance of the contract.

In the above example, if, at a later stage, Manish sells the flat to another person,

Sheetal, who purchases the same without knowledge of the agreement between Manish and Rita, she will get protection under the principle of part performance.

The doctrine of part performance does not apply to movable property.

9

Transfer Of Property To An Unborn Person

MEANING

A transfer of property to an unborn person, is a transfer by virtue of which an interest is created for the benefit of a person who is not in existence at the time of the transfer.

However, the law does not allow a transfer to be made directly to an unborn person. Therefore, an interest in the property is created in favour of another person on behalf of the unborn person.

Importantly, the interest that is created for the benefit of such a person must contain the whole of the remaining interest in the property of the person who desires to transfer the property. Otherwise such a transfer will not take effect.

■ Example : Amar (75) intends to transfer property to the son of Bijoy who is not in existence at the time of the transfer. Amar therefore, creates an interest in the property in favour of Bijoy, to hold the property on behalf of and as trustee for his unborn son. This transfer is valid only when the whole of the remaining interest of Amar will go to the benefit of the unborn person.

ROLE OF THE TRUSTEE

An interest created in favour of the unborn person follows a prior interest created in favour of another. It is this other person in whom the property vests, from the time an interest is created in favour of the unborn person till such time as the unborn person comes into existence. He acts as a trustee of the property.

Part 3

Corporate Matters

1

Types Of Companies

A Company is a voluntary association of persons who have come together for a common purpose.

TYPES

PRIVATE COMPANY

A private company is one which has a minimum paid-up capital of Rs. one lakh or as otherwise prescribed. The right to transfer the shares held by the shareholders of a private company are restricted. It can have a maximum of 50 members which do not include its employees-present or past. A minimum of two directors are required. The ordinary public is prohibited from subscribing to the shares or debentures of the company. So also, a private company is prohibited from accepting deposits from outsiders. The minimum number of persons required to start a private company are two.

PUBLIC COMPANY

A public company has a minimum paid up capital of Rs. 5,00,000/- or higher capital, as may be prescribed. A public company may or may not be listed at the stock exchange. The minimum number of persons required to start a public company are seven and it must have at least three directors. Unlike a private company, it is open for the general public who can subscribe to the shares of the company.

HOLDING AND SUBSIDIARY COMPANY

A company is said to be a holding company of another, when it has control over another company. The company over which control is exercised is the subsidiary company.

A company (for example company A) is said to be the subsidiary of another (Company B-the holding company) when the other company (i.e. company B) controls the composition of the board of directors of company A.

So also, when a holding company (Company X) has a subsidiary (Company Y) and company Z (another company) is a subsidiary of company Y, then company Z becomes a subsidiary of company X.

GOVERNMENT COMPANY

A company in which not less than 51% of the paid-up share capital is held by the Central or the State Government is known as a government company.

STATUTORY COMPANY

Companies which are created by and under an Act of Parliament, such as the Life Insurance Corporation of India under the LIC Act, or the Reserve Bank of India under the RBI Act, are statutory companies. In other words, these are companies which are created by and under a statute (law).

FOREIGN COMPANY

A foreign company is one which is incorporated (formed) outside India and has an established place of business within India.

A foreign company which establishes a place of business in India must, within 30 days, submit to the Registrar of Companies, a certified copy of documents including its Memorandum and Articles of Association, a list of its directors etc. At the time of issue of prospectus, a foreign company must state its country of incorporation.

COMPANIES FORMED FOR RELIGIOUS AND CHARITABLE PURPOSES

When a company is to be formed for religious or charitable purposes or for promoting art, science or commerce and intends to apply its profits for the promotion of these purposes, the Central Government grants it certain exemptions that would otherwise apply to limited companies. These companies may be registered without the words Limited or Private Limited.

2
Incorporation

There are various acts that need to be performed prior to the incorporation of a company. These acts are mandatory.

A. REGISTRATION

Before a company is incorporated, it needs to be registered.

The documents stated below need to be filed with the Registrar of Companies for the State in which the registered office of the company is to be situated. These documents also need to be duly stamped.

The Memorandum of Association of the Company contains:

a. name of the company, once it has been approved by the Registrar.

b. the state in which the registered office of the company is to be situated

c. the main objects and the ancillary objects of the company.

d. if it is a company having a share capital, it must also state the amount of share capital with which the company is to be registered and the number of shares that it is to be subdivided into.

e. the Memorandum shall be signed by seven or more persons in case of a public company or by two or more, in case of a private company. These people are the *subscribers*. The signatures must be attested by at least one witness, who is not a subscriber.

The Articles of Association of a Company :

The articles contain the various rules and regulations that have to be followed by the employees of the company. It serves as guideline for the management of its internal affairs. These guidelines may relate to:

a. share capital of the company.
b. transfer of shares.
c. forfeiture of Shares.
d. alteration of Capital.
e. voting rights of the members.
f. remuneration, qualifications and appointment of directors.
g. dividends and reserves.
h. manager
i. secretary
j. winding up etc.

- Agreement/s, if any executed by the company with any individual for appointment as its managing or full-time director or a manager.
- A list of people who have agreed to be the first directors of the company along with their written consent to act as directors of the company.
- A declaration stating that all the formalities required to be completed prior to registration have been complied with. The declaration must be signed by any of the following persons:
    a. an advocate of the Supreme Court or High Court.
    b. attorney or pleader who is entitled to appear before the High Court.
    c. company secretary or a chartered accountant, who practices full-time in India.
    d. person named in the Articles of Association of the company as the director, manager or secretary of the company.

B. CERTIFICATE OF INCORPORATION

Once all the above mentioned documents have been filed with the Registrar and the Registrar is satisfied that all the documents are in order, and that all the formalities have been complied with, he may then register the company and issue the Certificate of Incorporation of that company.

If he finds any minor defects or irregularities in the documents filed by the company, he can ask for them to be rectified. However, if the errors are substantial, then he has grounds to refuse registration of the company.

The Certificate of Incorporation is similar to a birth certificate. It signifies that all the formalities required for registration of a company have been complied with.

Once the Registrar issues the Certificate of Incorporation in the registered name of the company, the company comes into existence and becomes a legal entity by itself.

If the company is a private limited company it has the right to commence business once it obtains the Certificate of Incorporation. However, this is not the case with a public limited company. A public limited company is required to obtain a Certificate of Commencement of business, before it can commence business.

3

Meetings

The types of meetings attended by the shareholders of a company are as under:

(1) STATUTORY MEETING

Every company limited by shares and every company limited by guarantee and which has a share capital must hold a general meeting of the members of the company.

The meeting is to be held between the first and sixth month, from the date on which the company is entitled to start its business.

The board of directors of the company must forward a report known as the Statutory Report to every member of the company at least 21 days before the date fixed for the meeting.

The Statutory report sets out:

(a) the total number of *shares* that have been allotted.
(b) the total *cash* received in respect of the shares that have been allotted.
(c) an extract of the *receipts and payments* made by the company.
(d) the names of the *directors and auditors* of the company.
(e) the details of any *contract* which is to be submitted to the meeting for its approval.

This is the first meeting of the company. By forwarding the statutory report, the members have the opportunity to study beforehand and then discuss at the meeting, the contents of the report.

2. ANNUAL GENERAL MEETING (AGM)

Every company must, in each year, hold a general meeting, as its annual general meeting. The notice informing of such a meeting must specify that it is an annual general meeting. This meeting will be held in addition to any other meetings held by the company.

Not more than 15 months should separate two annual general meetings.

Place of the meeting: the meeting must be held in the registered office of the company or at some place within the city or town where the registered office of the company is located.

It is in this meeting that the shareholders of the company can question the working of the company.

Central Government : if a default is made by the company in holding the annual general meeting the Central Government may call or direct the calling of such a meeting.

3. EXTRA ORDINARY GENERAL MEETING

The directors of the company must, on the requisition of a certain number of members of the company, immediately proceed to call an extraordinary general meeting of the company.

Contents of the requisition:

The requisition made by the members must:

- specify the reasons for which the meeting is called.
- be signed by the requisitionists (persons making the requisition).
- be deposited at the registered office of the company.

If the board of directors does not, within 21 days from deposit of a requisition, call a meeting on a day not later than 45 days (from deposit of a requisition) the meeting may be called by the requisitionists themselves.

4

Resolutions

When a motion is accepted, it becomes a Resolution. A motion is a proposal that is placed for discussion in a meeting.

TYPES OF RESOLUTIONS

(A) Ordinary resolution

(B) Special resolution

(C) Resolutions that require special notice.

ORDINARY RESOLUTION

In a general meeting, when the number of votes cast in favour of a resolution exceeds the number of votes cast against the resolution, it is an ordinary resolution.

The votes of all the members that are present in the meeting and those represented by a proxy along with the casting vote of the chairman of the meeting, if any, are taken into consideration to ascertain the majority.

Instances when an ordinary resolution is needed:

1. appointment of a managing director/full time director.
2. adoption of a statutory report.
3. issuing of shares at a discounted rate.
4. alteration of the share capital.

5. appointment of auditors and fixation of their remuneration.

■ Example : Reliant Company Ltd., has 500 registered members. In the general meeting all the 500 members were present. 300 members voted in favour of a resolution and 200 voted against it. The resolution has been accepted by a simple majority i.e. the votes in favour of the motion are more than the votes against it, therefore it is an ordinary resolution.

SPECIAL RESOLUTION

The characteristics of a special resolution are:

1. the intention of proposing a resolution as a special resolution must be mentioned in the notice calling for the general meeting.
2. notice of such a general meeting must be duly given.
3. the number of votes cast in favour of the resolution must not be less than three times the vote cast against the Resolution.

Instances when a special resolution is needed:

1. alteration of the Articles of a company.
2. reduction of share capital.
3. payment of interest from the capital.
4. winding up of a company voluntarily.
5. variation of shareholders' right.

■ Example : Reliant Industries Ltd. has 800 registered members. The company felt a need to change its Articles of Association and decided to call a general meeting. It issued a notice for the same. The notice contained a proposal for a resolution to alter the Articles of Association. All 800 members were present for the meeting. When the motion was put on the floor for voting, 700 members voted in favour and the others voted against it. The motion is now a resolution. But since the votes cast in favour of it are more than three times the number of votes cast against it, it is now called a special resolution.

RESOLUTIONS REQUIRING SPECIAL NOTICE

A notice proposing such a resolution at a particular meeting, is to be given to the company, at least 14 days before such a meeting is to take place.

On receipt of the notice, the company, by turn, is required to give notice of the proposed resolution to its members in the same manner as it gives notice of a meeting.

Instances when a resolution of this nature is needed:

1. for the appointment of an auditor, other than the retiring ones.
2. for provisions against re-appointing a retiring auditor.
3. the Articles may further provide for any additional matters, when such special notice is required.

Registration of Resolutions

Generally, a copy of a resolution must be filed with the Registrar of Companies within 30 days of it being passed. The resolution should also be signed by an officer of the company.

5

Shares

A share is a single unit of the share capital of a company. Share Capital refers to the total amount of funds that have been collected on issuance of the company's shares. Shares are movable property transferable in the manner provided by the Articles of the company. Each share has a distinctive number.

TYPES OF SHARES

(A) Preference Shares

Preference shares are shares whose shareholders are:
(1) the first to receive dividends at the end of the year.
(2) the first to whom capital is returned at the time of winding up.

Preference shares may be :

(1) cumulative
(2) non-cumulative
(3) participating
(4) non-participating
(5) convertible
(6) non-convertible
(7) redeemable

(B) Equity Shares

Equity shares are those shares of a limited company having a share capital which are not preference shares.

Share Certificate

When a person holds shares he needs to have proof of ownership of the shares. For this purpose a company issues a share certificate in the name of the person holding the shares. It is a document which evidences the title of the share holder. The certificate is issued under the common seal of the Company. It specifies the name of the holder, the share certificate number, the distinctive numbers of the shares and the nominal value of each share. A duplicate share certificate can be issued if one is lost, destroyed, torn or mutilated.

Share Warrant

A public company limited by shares, if authorized by its Articles and with the previous approval of the Central Government, can issue under its common seal a Warrant in respect of its fully paid up shares. The warrant must state that the person bearing it is entitled to the shares specified therein. Shares can be transferred by mere delivery of the warrant.

Application and Allotment of Shares

An application is said to be made when a person intends to purchase a specific amount of shares of a company and for this purpose, makes an *application* to the company.

An allotment is when a company, after examining the application of a person *accepts* it and *allots* to the person, shares of the company.

Transfer of shares

Transfer of Shares refers to a change in the ownership of the shares. The company must acknowledge this change in ownership in their member's register. The transfer can be registered only on the execution of a proper instrument, duly stamped, between the transferor and the transferee. The Articles of Association of the company provides for the method of transfer to be followed.

- The board of directors has the right to refuse registration of a transaction of transfer and they need not specify any reason for it.

Nomination

A person holding shares of any company has the right to nominate a person who will be entitled to the shares in case of death of the present holder. A nomination can also be made by joint holders wherein they jointly nominate a person who will receive the ownership of the shares in the event of the death of all the joint holders. The transfer will take effect only on the death of the person/s making the nomination i.e. present holder/s. A minor can also be appointed as a nominee, provided the present holder of the shares makes a nomination to appoint another person, who will be entitled to the shares during the minority of the nominee.

Transmission

When a person becomes entitled to shares of any company through nomination he has two options:

(1) to accept the shares and get himself registered as a member with the company; or
(2) to transfer those shares in a manner similar to what the deceased holder/s would have done.

Transmission differs from transfer in two ways.

Firstly, transmission takes effect by operation of law.

■ Example : Dilip holds 100 shares of Kothari Chemicals Ltd. and has nominated Mihir as his nominee i.e. the person who shall be entitled to the shares in the event of his death. On the death of Dilip, Mihir is entitled to the said shares and has the option of either accepting these and becoming a registered member of the company, or transferring these shares in the same manner in which Dilip would have transferred them, had he been alive.

Secondly, there is no consideration involved in transmission.

6

Buy-Back of Shares & Employee Stock Option Scheme

B∪Y-BACK OF SHARES

Buy-back of shares is a process whereby a company buys back its own shares and other securities.

A company has the option to purchase its own shares and securities out of:

1. its free reserves i.e. reserves that have not been set apart for any specific purpose like general reserve.
2. its securities premium account.
3. the proceeds of any shares or other specified securities.

CONDITIONS

No company can purchase its own shares or securities unless:

1. the buy-back is authorized by the Articles of Association of the company.
2. a special resolution has been passed in the general meeting of the company authorizing the buy-back of shares.
3. the amount of shares or securities bought back are less than 25% of the total paid up capital and free reserves of the company.
4. the ratio of the debt owed by the company is not more than twice the

amount of the share capital and free reserves after the buy-back.
5. all the shares and other specified securities of the company are fully paid up.
6. the buy-back is in accordance with the regulations and guidelines issued by SEBI. (Securities Exchange Board of India)

MODES OF BUY-BACK

A company buy-back may be:

1. from its existing security holders.
2. from the open market.
3. where the company buys back shares that have been issued to its employees under the Employees' Stock Option Scheme. (ESOP)

CIRCUMSTANCES PROHIBITING BUY-BACK

A company cannot buy-back its own shares or other securities:

1. through any subsidiary company, including its own subsidiary company.
2. through an investment company or a group of investment companies.
3. if the company has defaulted in:
   (i) repayment of deposit or interest.
   (b) redemption of debentures or preference shares.
   (c) payment of dividend to any shareholder.
   (d) repayment of its loans or interest (on the loan) payable to any financial institution/bank and if the default is subsisting.

Employees Stock Option Scheme (ESOP)

ESOP is an option that is available to full time directors, officers and employees of a company giving them a right to purchase or to subscribe at a future date, the securities offered by the company.

Such securities are available to them at a predetermined price.

It is not compulsory for all the employees of a company to participate in such a scheme. There is a limit on the number of shares that an employee is entitled to.

7

Directors

Directors of a company play a vital role in the functioning of the company.

A public company must have at least three directors. Where a public company has a paid-up capital of Rs. five crores or more and having one thousand or more small share holders, the share holders may elect a director.

A private company must have two directors.

Collectively, the directors of a company are known as the Board of Directors. A company may increase or reduce the number of directors in a general meeting by passing an ordinary resolution.

Only an individual can be appointed as a director of a company. A limited company or partnership firm etc. cannot be a director of a company.

ROLES OF DIRECTORS

As agents

A company cannot act on its own. It has to act/contract through its representatives. The directors of the company represent the company. Directors are in charge of running the company business.

As trustees

The directors of the company are its trustees since they generally control the money, property etc. of the company. They also have several powers entrusted to them, such as, approving transfer of shares etc.

QUALIFICATIONS

A director must be of capable of entering into a contract and must have the necessary share qualification.

DISQUALIFICATIONS

A person is not capable of being appointed a director if:

(1) he is of unsound mind.
(2) he is an insolvent.
(3) he has been convicted by a court for any offence involving moral turpitude and has been imprisoned for not less than six months.
(4) he has not paid the calls in respect of the shares of the company held by him.

ADDITIONAL DIRECTORS

The board of directors has the power to appoint additional directors. These can be in office up to the date of the next annual general meeting of the company. Also, the number of directors and additional directors cannot exceed the maximum number of directors as fixed in the Articles of Association of the company.

NUMBER OF DIRECTORSHIPS

A person cannot, at one time, be a director in more than 15 companies.

REMOVAL OF A DIRECTOR

A director of a company may be removed by an ordinary resolution. A special notice is necessary to remove a director or to appoint a director in place of the director, so removed. It is the duty of the company to send a copy of the notice of the resolution to the director. The director has a right to be heard before he is removed from his office.

BOARD MEETINGS

Every company must have a meeting of its board of directors, once in three months. At least four meetings must be held in a year.

POWERS EXERCISED BY THE BOARD

The powers of the board of directors on behalf of the company include:

(1) the power to make calls to shareholders in respect of unpaid money on the shares.

(2) the power to issue debentures.

(3) the power to invest funds of the company.

(4) the power to grant loans etc.

These powers can be exercised only by means of a resolution passed during board meetings.

8

Other Managerial Personnel

(I) MANAGING DIRECTOR

A Managing Director is one on whose shoulder substantial managerial responsibilities lie.

The managerial responsibilities may be conferred on him by an agreement with the company, or a resolution passed in the general meeting of the company or through the Articles and Memorandum of Association of the company.

The power to alter or vary the responsibilities of a managing director lies with the company or its board of directors.

Restriction

A person shall not hold more than two managing directorships at the same time.

Disqualification

Disqualifications of managing directors are similar to those of a director.

Term of Office

The maximum number of years for which a managing director may hold office is 5 years.

A managing director is eligible for *reappointment,* and his term may be extended for another 5 years. There is *no limit* as to how many times a managing director may be reappointed.

The only restriction is that such an order for reappointment must not have been sanctioned two years before the date of expiration, of the present term of 5 years.

■ Example : Mr. Shah is appointed as the managing director of a company in 2000. He will be eligible of reappointment in 2005. A resolution sanctioning the reappointment will not be passed earlier than 2003.

(II) MANAGER

A manager is a person who manages and supervises all the affairs of the company. The manager works under the supervision and direction of the Board of Directors. He is answerable to the Board of Directors.

- A firm or a company cannot be appointed as manager.

Remuneration

A manager may either receive remuneration by way of a monthly payment or by way of a specified percentage of the net profits of the company.

Number of companies in which a person may be appointed as manager

A person may be appointed as manager of not more than two companies at any time, unless permitted by an order of the Central Government.

(III) COMPANY SECRETARY

A company secretary is a person who is a member of the Institute of Company Secretaries of India.

- Any person who is qualified to perform the duties which would otherwise have been performed by a company secretary can also be a company secretary.

A secretary performs various important managerial and ministerial functions. A secretary may be penalized if he is unable to execute his mandatory obligations towards the company.

Appointment

A secretary may be appointed by the Board of Directors. He may be also appointed through the Articles of Association. His appointment must be confirmed through a resolution passed in the first meeting of the Board of Directors that takes place after his appointment.

Qualifications

The qualifications required for appointment as a company secretary include:

(1) membership of the Institute of Company Secretaries of India, or

(2) a university degree in law, or

(3) a post graduate degree in commerce, or

(4) membership of the Institute of Chartered Accountants of India, or

(5) membership of the Institute of Cost and Works Accountants of India, or

(6) a post graduate degree in management studies.

9

Amalgamation

Amalgamation is a combination, union or merger. Under this topic we are limiting ourselves to amalgamation which can be either:

(a) by the transfer of one or more companies into a new company or,

(b) by the transfer of one or more companies into an existing company.

The company in which whole or part of business, property or liabilities is transferred to is called the *transferee company*. The company whose whole or part of business ie assets/liabilities is being transferred to the transferee company is called the *transferor company*.

PROCEDURE FOR AMALGAMATION

- Application to the court

An application has to be made to the court for sanctioning a (proposed) compromise or arrangement between the companies.

- The court may pass an order either sanctioning the compromise, or arrangement or by subsequent order make provisions for all or any of the matters including:

    (i) the transfer to the transferee company, in whole or any part of the property or liabilities of the transferor company.

    (ii) the allotment or appropriation by the transferee company of any shares, debentures, policies or other interest.

(iii) the continuation by or against the transferee company of any legal proceedings pending by or against the transferor company

(iv) the dissolution without winding up of the transferor company

(v) the provision to be made for any persons who disputes the compromise or arrangement.

(vi) such incidental, important and supplemental matters as are necessary to secure that the compromise or arrangement will be fully and successfully carried out.

REPORT OF COMPANY LAW BOARD OR THE REGISTRAR

Before approving a compromise or proposed arrangement, the court must receive a report from the Company Law Board or the Registrar, stating that the company has not been conducting its business in a manner detrimental to the interests of its members or to public interest.

REPORT OF OFFICIAL LIQUIDATOR

The court shall not pass an order for closure of any transferor company unless, on examination of the books and papers of the company, the Official Liquidator has sent a report to the court, stating that the company has been conducting its business in a manner harmful to the interests of its members or to public interest.

TRANSFER OF ANY PROPERTY OR LIABILITIES

Once an order is passed for transfer of the assets/liabilities, then the assets/liabilities of the transferor company will become those of the transferee company as per the order.

REGISTRATION

Every company, in relation to which the order is issued, must file a certified copy of such order with the Registrar of Companies for registration within 30 days from the time it is passed.

NOTICE TO CENTRAL GOVERNMENT

The court must notify the Central Government of every application it receives, and take into consideration the representation, if any made by the government before passing any order.

DISSENTING SHAREHOLDER

A dissenting shareholder includes a shareholder who, (1) has not consented to the scheme or contract or (2) has failed or refused to transfer his shares to the transferee company.

A scheme or contract involving the transfer of shares or any class of shares in a transferor company must be approved by holders of not less than nine-tenth in value of shares, within four months after making an offer on the behalf of the transferee company.

The transferee company may within two months after the expiry of four months give notice to the dissenting shareholder expressing its desire to acquire his shares.

The dissenting shareholder may file an application to the court within one month from the time such notice was given and the court will pass orders, as it thinks fit. When no application is made or the court refuses the same, the transferee company will become entitled and bound to acquire shares of the dissenting shareholder/s on the terms under the scheme or contract by which the shares of approving shareholders are transferred.

AMALGAMATION IN NATIONAL INTEREST

The Central Government may pass an order notified in the official gazette, providing for amalgamation of the two or more companies into a single company, where it is satisfied that it is essential in public interest to do so.

Such an order may provide the constitution of the company with such property, powers, rights, interest, authorities and privileges and with such liabilities, duties as may be specified.

Also, such an order may provide for the continuation of any legal proceedings by or against the transferee company pending by or against any transferor company.

Every member or creditor (including debenture holders) of each of the companies, before amalgamation, will have the same interest in or rights against the company, as resulting from the amalgamation. If his interest is reduced, he is entitled to compensation which must be paid by the company resulting from the amalgamation. Any member aggrieved by the assessment of compensation may prefer an appeal to the Company Law Board.

10

Winding Up Of A Company

Winding up refers to the commencement of proceedings that would result in the closure of the company and its business.

There are three ways in which a company may wind up:

I. by court orders.
II. voluntarily.
III. subject to the supervision of the court.

I. WINDING UP BY THE COURT

This takes place in the following circumstances:

- when the company has, by a special resolution, resolved that the company should be wound up by the court.
- when the company has defaulted in delivering the statutory report to the Registrar of Companies or in the holding of the statutory meeting of the company.
- when the company does not commence its business within one year of its incorporation or when it suspends its business for a year;
- when the number of the members of the company is less than two, in case of a private company or seven, in case of a public company.
- when the company is unable to pay its debts.

- when, in the opinion of the court, it is just and equitable to wind up the company.

A petition for winding up may be presented to the court by either:

- the company
- the creditor/s of the company
- the Registrar of companies.
- the parties mentioned in the aforesaid three points, either together or separately; or
- any person authorized by the Central Government.

II. VOLUNTARY WINDING UP

A company may be voluntarily wound up in the following circumstances:

- when the period, if any, fixed for the duration of the company by the Articles, has expired and a resolution has been passed in the general meeting requiring the company to be wound up voluntarily.
- when an event, if any, has occurred, of which the Articles state that the company is to be dissolved and a resolution has been passed in the general meeting requiring the company to be wound up voluntarily; or
- when the company has passed a special resolution requiring the company to wind up voluntarily.

Voluntary winding up commences at the time when the resolution for it is passed.

Once the resolution has been passed, the company must give notice of the resolution by advertisement in the official gazette and also in a newspaper that is circulated in the district in which the registered office of the company is situated. The notice must be given within fourteen days of the passing of the resolution.

The company to be wound up shall cease to carry on its business from the commencement of voluntary winding up proceedings.

III. SUBJECT TO THE SUPERVISION OF THE COURT

At any time after a company has passed a resolution for voluntary winding up, the court has the right to pass an order, stating that such voluntary winding up shall continue under the supervision of the court.

The winding up shall continue on the terms and conditions as decided by the court.

A petition for continuance of voluntary winding up will be treated in the same way as a petition for winding up by court, for the purpose of determining the jurisdiction of the court over the legal proceedings.

Specimen of a Winding up notice

By REGISTERED A.D.

ABC Pvt. Ltd.
ABC House,
_____.

(sent at the registered office address)

Dear Sirs,

    RE: PAYMENT OF DUES OF _____.

We are addressing this letter on behalf of our client, _____, as under:

1. We are instructed that:-

   a. Pursuant to Orders placed by you on our client, in Bombay it sold, supplied and delivered to you (goods) of the value of Rs. _____ in or about _____ and raised on you various bills in respect thereof as per Annexure A.

   b. You duly received the said goods and bills, without raising any dispute relating to the quality or quantity of the goods supplied or the rates charged.

   c. Despite requests, you have wrongfully failed and neglected to pay the said sum of Rs. _____ or any part thereof.

2. In the premises our client hereby calls upon you to pay the said sum of Rs._____/- with interest thereon at the rate of 18% p.a. from the date of receiving this Notice till payment.

3. If you fail to pay the said amount along with interest for a period of three weeks from the date of the receipt of this notice, you will be deemed to be unable to pay your debts and our client will initiate recovery proceedings including winding up proceedings against the Company at its risk, cost and account.

4. Please treat this as a Notice under section 434 of the Companies Act.

Yours faithfully,

Enclosure :a/a

Part IV
Criminal Matters

1

Cheque Dishonour

A cheque is a Bill of Exchange drawn on a specific bank and is not payable other than on demand.

Most of us make payments by cheques for various purposes. This is to draw the attention of the reader to the offence of bouncing of cheques, the reasons for which the cheque drawn is returned unpaid by the bank and the consequences that follow.

When any cheque drawn by a person (having an account with a bank) for payment of any amount of money to another out of that account for discharge in whole or in part of any debt or other liability, is returned by the bank unpaid, either because the money in the account is insufficient or it exceeds the amount arranged to be paid (by an agreement made with the bank), the cheque is dishonoured.

Punishment: A person will be punished with imprisonment upto 2 years or fine which may extend upto twice the amount of the cheque or both.

CONDITIONS FOR LIABILITY

(1) The cheque must be presented to the bank within six months from the date it was drawn or within its validity, whichever is earlier.

(2) The payee (in whose favour the cheque is drawn) makes a demand for payment of the said amount of money. The demand must be made by giving a

notice in writing to the drawer of the cheque, within 30 days of receipt of information from the bank, and

(3) The drawer fails to make the payment within 15 days of receipt of the notice.

On non-payment of the due amount, a complaint should be made by the payee within one month from the date of expiry, of the period of 15 days. The civil remedy of the complainant is not barred when he takes this recourse.

- If the cheque given by way of a gift or present is dishonoured by the bank the drawer is not liable.

PRESENTATION AND CAUSE OF ACTION

The apex court has held that there is no restriction upon the payee to present a dishonoured cheque any number of times, during the period of its validity. Once the notice is given the cause of action arises and the right to present the cheque again is lost.

COMPLAINT

A complaint must be in writing. It must be filed by a person who is capable of making a physical appearance in court. For instance, when the company is the complainant, it is necessary that an authorized person represents the company in court. In case the person committing an offence is a company, then every person (at the time of offence), who was in charge of and responsible to the company for the conduct of its business and the company will be liable. If the offence is proved to be committed by any individual person/s then such person/s will be proceeded against.

A copy of the returned cheque along with the bank's advice for return of cheque and a copy of the notice with proof of receipt must accompany the complaint. In certain cases, the courts have accepted complaints filed before the expiry of the period of 15 days when the money was not paid, even after the expiry of 15 days. A Metropolitan Magistrate or a Judicial Magistrate First Class has the authority to try this offence.

- Example : Ramesh Rangwalla issued a cheque for Rs.50,000/- dated 1.1.2004 drawn on Bank of India, M.G. Road Branch, Bombay in favour of Pradhan Mhatre, as payment for a computer and printer. Pradhan deposited the cheque with his bank i.e. Bank of Baroda on 7.1.2004 but the bank returned the same, dishonoured with an "advice" dated 10.1.2004 stating "funds insufficient". Pradhan gave a notice of dishonour and demand (by hand delivery) dated 14.1.2004 which was received by Ramesh on 16.1.2004 who failed to pay the amount within 15 days from 16.1.2004 and even thereafter. A cause of action or a right to file the complaint against Ramesh accrued on the expiration of the said period of 15 days and Pradhan became entitled to file a complaint within one month from the date of such expiration.

The prescribed time limit is vital. Let's see how. If Pradhan were to give the notices but not file the complaint within the said period of one month and instead present the cheque from time to time during its validity. If each time, Bank of Baroda were to return the cheque with the same advice "funds insufficient", before Pradhan finally decides to file a complaint for dishonour, the complaint would not be maintainable in law since Pradhan did not file the same within 30 days of the expiration of the period under the first notice, dated 14.1.2004.

The law protects the aggrieved party but he too must be vigilant in seeking legal redress.

REASONS FOR DISHONOUR OF A CHEQUE

These include lack of funds, account of the drawer being closed, cheque amount exceeds arrangement, drawer's signature differs, 'stop payment' instructions by drawer etc.

- A post-dated cheque becomes a cheque on the date written on it. Until then it is not payable. Therefore, a dishonour of a post-dated cheque does not arise since it cannot be presented to the Bank.

Cases

- *Liability of a Partner:* in a case filed against a partner of a firm, it was held

- *Failure to file complaint:* the complainant's lawyer sent a notice to the drawer when the cheque was returned by the bank due to insufficiency of funds. On receipt of the notice, the drawer requested the payee for some time to pay the amount but he failed to pay the same. In the meantime, the complainant did not file the complaint. After a few months, the complainant once again presented the cheque which was dishonoured and he sent a notice. On the drawer's failure to pay the amount, a complaint was filed. The same was dismissed as not maintainable.

REGISTERED A.D./COURIER

ABC Ltd.,

_____

_____

Dear sirs,

Re: Notice under section 138 of the negotiable instruments act.

We are addressing this letter on behalf of our client, XYZ Company Ltd. (Company), Mumbai, as under:

1. We are instructed that:

    a. Pursuant to Orders placed by you on the Company in Bombay, it sold, supplied and delivered to you Castor Seeds (goods) of the value of Rs. _____/- (Rupees _____ only) on or about April-May 2006 and raised on you bills in respect thereof as per Annexure A. The same were delivered to you in Bombay.

    b. You duly received the said goods and bills, without raising any dispute relating to the quality or quantity of the good supplied or the rates charged.

2. We are instructed that:

   a. In acknowledgement of your liability to pay the said billed amount, you issued cheques and delivered the same to our client Company, at Bombay, for an aggregate amount of Rs. _____/- (Rupees _____ only), in favour of our client, as part payment leaving a balance of a sum of Rs. _____/- (Rupees _____ only) due and payable by you to it as price of the goods sold. Detailed of the cheques issued are as Annexure B.

   b. In or about April-May, 2006 you issued cheques for Rs. _____/-. These cheques were signed by your Director and/or by the Principal Officer(s) if the Company, who are in charge of the day-to-day affairs and management of your Company. Our client Company deposited the same cheques with its Bank, _____, _____ Branch. These cheques were dishonoured.

   c. On request, your representative _____ arrived at our client Company's Bombay office at _____, Bombay at the said office that all the cheques shall be cleared on representation. These assurances were false as all the cheques were again dishonoured when deposited in the same bank. The bank advices are as per Annexure C.

   d. Out of these cheques the following cheques were again dishonoured as under:

      i. Cheques No. _____ of the amount of Rs. _____/-, returned by the bank on _____ and when deposited again was returned on _____ with the remark "Insufficient Funds".

      iii. Cheques No. _____ of the amount of Rs. _____/-, returned by the bank on _____ and when deposited again was returned on _____ with the remark "Insufficient Funds".

3. We are instructed that:

   a. You issued the said cheques to discharge your liability in part under the said bills and as debt due within the meaning of section 138 of the Negotiable Instruments Act.

   b. The whole transaction and discussions on the dishnourment and assurances took place in Bombay as aforesaid.

4. In the premises, our client Company hereby calls upon you to pay to it the said sum of Rs. _____/- with interest thereon at the rate of _____% p.a. from the date of receipt of this Notice till payment, representing the aggregatge amount of the dishonoured cheques.

5. This notice is given to you within 30 days of receiving the said bank advise as per enclosurea and Annexure C.

6. If you fail to pay the same within 15 days from the receipt hereto, our client Compnay will institute appropriate legal proceedings against you and against your Directors/Principal Officer(s) who are managing the day to day affairs of your Company.

                                                    Yours faithfully,

                                        For_____

2

Property Related Crimes

Property includes moveable and immoveable property. Moveable property includes physical property of every kind *except* land and things attached to the earth. Cars, animals, jewellery, crops are instances of moveable property.

Immoveable property includes land, buildings and things attached to the earth.

OFFENCES

The offences or crimes against property are of different kinds such as theft, robbery, extortion, cheating, criminal misappropriation and so on.

Theft

It is one of the most commonly seen offences. Any person who dishonestly takes any moveable property out of another person's possession without his permission, commits the offence of theft. The property must be moved from where it was originally.

To constitute this offence there must be a dishonest intention.

■ Example: Sanjay, an engineer by profession, takes off his shoes before entering the temple. After he completes his prayers he wears a pair of shoes thinking they are his own. He soon discovers that it was not his pair and promptly rushes to return them to the lawful owner. In this case Sanjay's act does not amount to theft as there was no dishonest intention on his part.

Apart from the element of dishonest intention, the property should be moveable. So also, the property must be taken away from the possession of the person without his permission and must be moved from the place it was originally.

Can a person be liable if he commits theft of his own property? The answer is yes, if he does so from someone who has responsibility to keep the same.

■ Example: Ajeeb Rathore has Rs.1,00,000/- in his savings a/c in a reputed bank. He attempts to steal that money from the bank saying that it belongs to. He is guilty of committing theft.

Extortion

When any person intentionally induces another, to deliver a person or property by threatening to injure him commits the offence of extortion. The offence extends to putting any person in fear or death or grave hurt.

■ Example: Balbir Kaur threatens to kill Raj Sinha's son unless he pays a sum of Rs.25 lakh to Kaur. Kaur is guilty of extortion.

Robbery

When death, hurt or wrongful restraint is caused to the victim while committing the offence of theft, it amounts to robbery.

When the offender at the time of committing extortion and being in the presence of the victim puts the victim in fear of death or hurt, the offence of robbery is committed.

Dacoity

When five or more persons jointly commit robbery, every person is said to commit dacoity.

Criminal misappropriation of property

Any dishonest misappropriation (embezzlement/misuse) or conversion (alteration) of any moveable property by a person for his own use is criminal misappropriation of property.

However, when a person finds property not in possession of another and takes it either for protecting it, or giving it back to the owner he is not liable. He will not be entitled to this benefit in case he had the means to find out the owner.

■ Example: Mr. D'souza a software engineer, was on his way home when he found a gold plated fountain pen at the office gate. He was not quite certain as to whether the pen belonged to his colleague. The next morning he made some enquiries and on discovering that the pen belonged to his colleague promptly handed it over to the rightful owner. Hence, Mr. D'souza is not guilty.

Stolen property : when possession of property is transferred by theft, extortion, robbery etc. it is known as stolen property. It is irrelevant whether the transfer has been made in or outside India

Receiving stolen property: Any person who dishonestly and intentionally receives stolen property is guilty of this offence.

Cheating

A person cheats when he deceives another and fraudulently and dishonestly induces him to part with any property to any person, or agrees that any person shall retain property knowing that this act could harm the person, (i.e. the victim), his reputation or property.

■ Example: Sumer Ali, an auctioneer has an auction of film memorabilia. He is aware that each of these articles are duplicates. Thus, Sumer Ali is a cheat.

When a person cheats by pretending to be some other person he is said to be guilty of cheating by Personation.

■ Example: Jaswinder Singh, in addition to being an aspiring actress is also a look alike of a Hindi film actress. She signs a contract with a south Indian ad-film company pretending to be the film personality she resembles. The company had no means to verify the same and believed her representation to be true when she submitted (false) proof. In a case filed against Jaswinder Singh for cheating, the company succeeded.

Criminal Trespass

Any person who either enters into or has already entered into the property of another, with the intention to insult or intimidate the person who is in possession of the property commits criminal trespass.

3

Counterfeiting

A person is said to 'counterfeit' when he causes one thing to resemble another, with the intention of deception. In other words, a counterfeit is an imitation to resemble that which is original.

Counterfeiting may take place in coins, seals, government stamps, as well as in trademarks. This is an offence recognized by the Indian Penal Code. Let us see the different types of offences under this category.

COINS

- Counterfeiting of coins : committing counterfeiting of any coin or any process relating to counterfeiting knowingly, is an offence.

- Counterfeiting of Indian coins: any person who counterfeits or knowingly performs any part of the process of counterfeiting Indian coins, shall be punished more severely than the offence mentioned above.

Possession by a person of any instrument or material for the purpose of using it for counterfeiting coins or having knowledge that such material is intended to be used for that purpose is an offence.

■ Example: Amarjit and his friends were in the process of counterfeiting coins to make quick money. As a result, each of them was to bring the necessary material and assemble at Amarjit's house. On a raid conducted by the police various forms of dyes, materials, instruments and tools were found. On questioning, Amarjit and his friends confessed to their offence and they were liable as such.

- Abetment : abetment by any person in India of counterfeiting any coins outside of India is punishable.
- Import/Export : whoever knowingly, imports into India or exports out of India, any counterfeit coins is punishable for the offence. Where the person is guilty of importing or exporting Indian coins, the punishment is more severe.
- Delivery of Coins: any person knowing that he has, in his possession, a counterfeit coin, and who fraudulently delivers it to another or induces another person to receive it, is liable to be punished. In the case of Indian coins, the accused will be dealt with more severely.
- Employee in a mint: when an employee in a mint does, or omits to do something, which he is legally bound to do, with the intention of causing the coin issued from the mint, to be of a different weight or composition than that fixed by law, he is liable for punishment.

■ Example : Ramesh Pillai was a supervisor at India Mint Factory, a mint established by the Government of India. Pillai's duty was to ensure that Rs. 5/- coins were to be of the specification fixed under the law. However, due to Pillai's negligence, defective coins that were not of the requisite specification, were passed. Hence, Pillai was guilty.

So also, any person who, without lawful permission, takes out of any mint (established in India), any tool or instrument used for the purposes of making coins is guilty.

- Tampering: any person who dishonestly performs any procedure on any coin which either has a result in altering its weight or composition is liable to be punished.

GOVERNMENT STAMPS

- Counterfeiting: whoever, counterfeits or performs any process of counterfeiting any revenue stamp, issued by the Government is liable to be punished.

- Making/Selling: any person who makes, buys or sells any instrument knowing that it is for the purpose of counterfeiting any stamp issued by the Government for revenue shall be punished.
- Reuse: any person who uses any stamp issued by the Government which he knows has been used before, shall also be punished.

4

Offences Relating To Religion

What is Religion?

Religion is a term easy to describe but difficult to define. In brief-religion is a faith. It is a system of faith and worship in different forms. It forms a very integral part of Indian culture. Temples, mosques, churches, holy rivers, are all *religious places*. Holy books such as the Koran, the Guru Granth Sahib are *religious objects*.

OFFENCES

The offences or wrongs against religion are committed in different forms and are of different types.

- Any person who destroys or damages any place of worship or any religious object shall be punished with imprisonment and fine or both. Provided :

    (a) the person does so with the intention of insulting the persons of that religion

    or

    (b) the person doing so has knowledge that such act of destruction or damage will insult the persons of that religion.

■ Example: Ravi and Sanjay visit a temple. They desecrate the holy book placed inside the temple room by tearing some of the pages. They are liable for this offence.

- Any person voluntarily causing disturbance to any gathering, which is lawfully engaged in the performance of religious worship or ceremonies can be punished with imprisonment, or fine or both.

To satisfy the conditions for this offence it is necessary that the person causing the disturbance must be doing so willingly of his own free accord. Also, the offence must be committed during the religious worship. It is important to note that the gathering must be legitimately engaged in the performance of their worship or ceremonies.

■ Example: In a village affected by drought and famine in Rajasthan, like every year, about 100 brahmins from Seva Kar Ashram got together to perform a maha yagna to appease the rain gods. The yagna was held on a ground meant for such purposes. A group of men who wanted to play cricket on the same ground couldn't do so. Dejected, they tried to disrupt the yagna by hurling stones at the brahmins. They were liable to be punished.

- Deliberate and cruel intention to outrage religious feelings: Any person with deliberate and cruel intention who outrages the religious feelings of any class of citizens of India either by words or by signs insults the religious belief of that class is liable.

■ Example: Supreme Films makes a film on the life of a holy saint, where he is depicted as a man driving the latest cars, wearing designer clothes and who is always in the company of young women. The film was taken off the theatres and the makers of the film were held liable.

- Promoting disharmony on grounds of religion - Any person who :

    (a) by words or signs promotes or attempts to promote enmity, hatred or disharmony between religious groups on grounds of religion, race, birth place, residence etc.,

    or

    (b) commits any act which is harmful to maintenance of peace between different religions or which disturbs public peace,

or

(c) organizes any movement in which the participants will use criminal force or be trained to use criminal force against any religious group which activity causes fear amongst the members of such religious community is liable to be punished.

The punishment is *more severe* if any of the above offences are committed in any place of worship or in any gathering/assembly engaged in the performance of religious worship.

- Allegations pertaining to national integration

Where any person by words or signs:

(a) makes a charge that any class of persons cannot, by reason of being members of any religious group etc., bear true faith and loyalty to the Constitution of India.

or

(b) asserts that that any class of persons by reason of being members of any religious group etc. be deprived of their rights as citizens of India – such a person shall be punished.

5

Forgery

A PERSON COMMITS FORGERY WHEN HE MAKES ANY FALSE DOCUMENT:

    (a)   intending to cause damage or injury to any person or to the public.

    (b)   to cause any person to part with property.

    (c)   to enter into an agreement with an intention to commit fraud *or*

Making false electronic records is also included.

HOW IS A FALSE DOCUMENT MADE?

A false document is made by a person (person 'A') who dishonestly makes, signs, seals or executes a document with the intention of having others believe that another person ('B') had made, signed etc. such document which he (i.e. A) knows that ('B') had not made, signed as such.

HOW IS A FALSE ELECTRONIC RECORD MADE?

A false electronic record is said to be made when any person dishonestly makes or transmits any electronic record, or attaches any digital signature on any electronic record, with the intention that it be believed that another person ('B') had made such record when he (i.e. A) knows that ('B') had not made it. Alteration of an electronic record without proper authority or dishonestly by a person is also included.

■ Example : The firm, Phiroz and Sons are wholesale dealers in textiles. Kishorilal, a retailer approached the firm to do business on a running account basis. When Kishorilal presented an invoice for Rs. 25,000/- the firm issued a cheque signed by the authorised signatory, for the same amount. Before depositing the cheque, Kishorilal fraudulently and dishonestly superimposed a larger amount and signed it as though it had been signed by the authorised signatory of the firm. Kishorilal is guilty of this offence.

WHEN A PERSONS OWN SIGNATURE AMOUNTS TO FORGERY

When a person signs his own name on a document (for instance : by drawing a cheque) intending it to be believed, that it was drawn by another person, he is said to have committed forgery.

DEAD PERSON

The offence of forgery is also committed when a person makes a false document in the name of a dead person intending everyone to believe that the deceased person made the document during his lifetime.

PUNISHMENT FOR THE OFFENCE OF FORGERY

Whoever, commits the offence of forgery shall be punished with imprisonment, which may extend upto 2 years, or with fine or both.

COURT OR PUBLIC RECORDS

When a document which is either a (1) record of a court of justice, (2) birth register (3) marriage certificate, (4) Power of Attorney, (5) any public document made by a public officer in his official capacity or any other such document, is forged by a person, then such person is liable for the offence of forgery. In this case, the punishment may extend up to 7 years.

Forgery of another person's will is also an offence.

■ Example : In the year 1995, five brothers of Zaveri family purchased a flat in their joint names. Since all four brothers, but Shamsher had their own separate flats, they agreed that Shamsher will reside in the above flat. In or around the year 2001, disputes within the family took place. However, Shamsher continued to reside in the above flat. He decided to sell the flat without the knowledge of his brothers. Shamsher made and signed four different Power of Attorneys on behalf of his brothers as though they were executed by them in his favour, authorizing him to sell the flat. Shamsher has committed forgery.

DEFAMATION

When a person commits forgery with intention that the document or electronic record so forged will harm the reputation of another, he is liable to be punished.

ACCOUNTS

When a clerk or any person who is acting as a clerk or a servant, willfully and with an intention to defraud, either destroys, alters, falsifies any book, writing, accounts belonging to his employer or helps any person in this regard, is also guilty of this offence.

PROPERTY MARK

A property mark is one, which shows that certain moveable property belongs to a particular person.

Where a person has moveable property, goods, case or package which he marks in a manner, which causes others to believe the property, goods, case or package so marked belong to a person (Company etc.), to whom actually they do not actually belong, such person uses a false property mark.

■ Example : Rasiklal & Sons are retailers of coconut oil. On each bottle and the packages containing the bottles, they stamp the word "Parachute", thereby causing the consumers to believe that the coconut oil sold by Rasiklal & Sons belong to the brand "Parachute" when it is actually not so. Rasiklal & Sons are guilty of using a false property mark.

6

Crimes Against Women

Women today are victims of molestation, eve teasing, rape etc. in the office, in college, on the streets or even at home. This is the situation in the metropolitans as well as in rural areas. In fact, in the rural areas, the instances are more.

A recent article published in a newspaper described how a married woman from a village in central India was subjected to all forms of third degree torture which included beating, being paraded naked and stoned and ultimately being locked up by the villagers. The reason for this is unimaginable. She accused her husband of having an affair with another woman. Yes, this is barbaric and depicts the sorry state of affairs in this country. In metropolitan cities, women are more aware of their rights and can approach the enforcement agencies to obtain redress.

Let us now look at some such offences

RAPE

A man who has sexual intercourse with a woman is said to commit rape when :

(1) it is against her will.
(2) without her consent.
(3) with her consent when it has been obtained by putting her or her near and dear ones in fear of death.
(4) with her consent when the man knows he is not her husband but she

believes that he is her husband.
(5) with her consent when she is unable to understand the nature of her act by reason of being intoxicated or of unsound mind.
(6) when she is under 16 year of age - with or without her consent.

Sexual intercourse by a man with his own wife, who is over 15 years of age is not rape. However, when a man has intercourse with his wife when they are living separately it will be rape.

The offence is more serious when rape has been committed by a police officer on a woman in his custody or by the hospital staff on a woman in that hospital.

OFFENCES RELATING TO MARRIAGE

- When a man, by deceit causes a woman (not his wife) to believe that she is lawfully married to him and has sexual inter course with her he shall be punished.
- Marriage by a husband during the life time of his wife is an offence on the part of the husband. In any case, such a marriage is invalid. This applies to the wife as well.

CRUELTY AGAINST WOMEN

- When the husband (or his relative) subjects a woman to cruelty he shall be punished with imprisonment of upto three years, along with a fine.

Cruelty in this case means any act which drives the woman to commit suicide or to cause grave injury to herself.

It also includes harassment of a woman when she (or any person related to her) fails to meet any unlawful demand for any property or valuable security.

■ Example: Ravi Bajaj who is unemployed, is married to Mona who belongs to a rich family. Along with his parents, Ravi abuses her physically and once, even tries to burn her. Ravi and his parents have made threats and demands for money and jewellery to Mona. On a police complaint filed by Mona against her husband and in-laws, the police are justified in taking action against them.

DOWRY DEATH

When the death of a woman is caused by burns or any bodily injury, or occurs other than under natural circumstances within seven years of marriage, it amounts to dowry death if it can be proved that soon before her death, she was subjected to cruelty or harassment by her husband (or his relative) for or in connection with dowry.

The husband or relative shall be guilty of causing her death.

Note:
 (1) Death of a woman caused by suicide is not death under normal circumstances.
 (2) The prosecution should establish a direct connection between the death of the woman and a demand for dowry.
 (3) The cruelty must be continuous leading unto the death of the woman.

CRUELTY AT WORK

The working woman is often subjected to and is a victim of sexual harassment at work. Sexual harassment includes:

 (a) physical contact by her male counterparts including seniors.
 (b) demanding sexual favours from the woman who is under constant threat of losing her job.
 (c) any other humiliating statement or remark which constitutes a health and safety problem for the woman.

■ Example : Preeti Singh 21, had taken up a job at Alcons Software. It was a custom that the current employees will play a prank on the new employee. As the managing partner was not in office, the employees decided that one amongst them, would act as a partner in front of Preeti and ask her to type an official letter. This is not a case of sexual harassment.

Our Constitution provides for just and humane conditions for work and makes it an enforceable right if these conditions are not observed.

It is the duty of the employer or persons in charge at work places to prevent the commission of sexual harassment as well as to provide remedial measures for the same. Recourse to the Court of Law is open.

7

Murder & Culpable Homicide

The Right to Life is a fundamental right given to us by the Constitution. Not only in India, but throughout the world, this right is well respected.

We often make a mistake in understanding the implications of the term *murder*. Before we discuss this let us understand the term *homicide*.

Homicide is a Latin word. The word Homa means 'man' and Cide means 'cut' - which means killing of one human being by other human being. It could be lawful as well as unlawful.

LAWFUL HOMICIDE

When a person exercises the right of self defence and kills another person or when death is caused by accident, it is lawful homicide.

UNLAWFUL HOMICIDE

This includes cases where culpable (i.e. blameworthy) homicide classifies as murder and where it does not classify as murder. To hold the person liable for culpable homicide amounting to murder the following elements should be present i.e.

- when a person causes the death of another with the intention to cause death *or*

- when a person causes such bodily injury to another with the intention to cause death of the other person *or*
- when a person does such act knowingly, which will cause the death of the other person.

■ Example : Maria and her five year old nephew Joseph were walking along the roadside. A speeding truck was coming from the opposite direction. Suddenly Maria pushed her nephew in front of the truck. The truck hit Joseph which resulted in his death. Maria was held liable for committing culpable homicide.

Maria knew that her act (i.e. pushing her nephew towards the truck) would be fatal to her nephew's life and her intention was to kill her nephew. Therefore, she is guilty.

A person ('A') who causes bodily injury to another ('B') who is suffering from disorder, disease or bodily infirmity and such injury results in death of that other person ('B') then he ('A') is said to have caused his death.

■ Example : Ram and Ravi are brothers. Ravi had a brain tumour and Ram was aware of it. A dispute arose between them regarding division of their ancestral property. Ram threw a wooden stick at Ravi's head which caused him multiple head injuries, and consequently, he died. Ram was held for committing culpable homicide because he knew that Ram already had a brain tumour. In normal circumstances such injuries may not have resulted in the death of a person of sound health.

- A person is said to have caused the death of another when he causes such bodily injury to other person, which resulted in his death although had he taken proper remedies, the life of that person could have been saved.

■ Example : An altercation took between Ajay & Brijen. Ajay strikes Brijen with a hockey stick due to which Brijen starts bleeding and falls unconscious for a reasonably long time. Nobody takes him to hospital. Ajay runs away from the place. Brijen dies two days later as he did not get treatment on time. Ajay was held liable for committing culpable homicide.

In this case, Ajay cannot say in his defence that Brijen's life could have been saved had he been hospitalized on time or his striking Brijen was not sufficient to cause the death of a person in normal circumstances.

DEATH OF A CHILD IN THE MOTHER'S WOMB

Causing the death of a child in the mother's womb is not homicide. But it may amount to culpable homicide to cause the death of a living child if any part of that child has been brought forth, though the child may not have breathed or been completely formed.

When the child is in the mother's womb, it is a part of his mother's life and therefore does not have a separate existence. Thus, while it is in the womb, causing death of such a child does not amount to homicide. If any part of that child, for instance a finger has been formed, the child will be regarded as full grown person. And therefore causing death of such a child will become a serious offence.

THE OFFENCE OF MURDER IS REDUCED TO CULPABLE HOMICIDE WHICH IS NOT MURDER UNDER:

I. GRAVE AND SUDDEN PROVOCATION

Being deprived of self-control and under grave and sudden provocation, causing the death of the person who agitated him or another person by mistake or by accident.

■ Example : Ram's wife had a clandestine affair with his neighbour Shyam. Pandu who was aware of this relation would tease Ram whenever he passed by his house. On one occasion, Pandu made fun of Ram in front of other villagers due to which Ram lost his temper and he beat Pandu to death. Ram was held liable for culpable homicide not amounting to murder, because Pandu was the cause of grave and sudden provocation to Ram due to which he lost self control and killed Pandu.

II. RIGHT OF PRIVATE DEFENCE

Exercise of the right to private defence in good faith, by a person which causes the death of another without any planning and any intention of doing more harm than necessary.

■ Example : Rana, entered Lalita's home when she was alone, with the intention to rape her. Lalita, to save herself stabbed Rana with a knife due to which he died. Lalita was justified in doing so as she was acting in self-defence.

However, when Ravi found a thief stealing his money he beat him violently till death. It cannot be argued that he acted with bonafide intention or in the exercise of his right of private defence. He will be guilty of murder.

III. SUDDEN FIGHT

A sudden fight or quarrel where no undue advantage is taken, or acting in a cruel manner are also circumstances where culpable homicide does not amount to murder.

■ Example : A quarrel took place between Sanju and Monu. Sanju strikes Monu with a bat. Monu, to save himself pushed Sanju against a wall due to which he sustained brain injuries and died. Monu will be liable for culpable homicide which does not amount to murder.

IV. PUBLIC SERVANT EXCEEDING HIS LEGAL POWERS

If a public servant exceeds his legal powers and thereby causes the death of the other person, without having any ill will towards that person, he will get the benefit of this provision.

V. VICTIM'S CONSENT

If the person killed is above 18 years and consents to his own death the case comes under this provision.

■ Example : Raju was suffering from lung cancer due to which he had suffered immensely. He therefore requested his father to kill him and relieve him from his agonies. One night, under frustration his father gave him poison due to which he died. His father will be held liable for culpable homicide not amounting to murder.

8
Words & Phrases

After having discussed some significant topics under this part let us look at certain relevant terms and their meanings that require mention:

PUBLIC SERVANTS

These include:
  (i) officers in the armed forces,
  (ii) judges, officers of a court, members of panchayat,
  (iii) arbitrators
  (iv) people who have the authority of law to keep any person in confinement,
  (v) government officers whose duty it is to prevent offences,
  (vi) persons who hold an office, by which they are empowered to conduct an election,
  (vii) persons who are in the service or pay of the government for the performance of any public duty.

Examples : (1) A Court Receiver is an officer of a court, (2) A Police officer, (3) Bus Conductor etc.

WRONGFUL GAIN AND WRONGFUL LOSS

When any person gains by illegal means, from any property to which he is not entitled, he is said to wrongfully gain.

The loss caused by unlawful means of property to the person (who is legally entitled to) but who is being deprived of it, is wrongful loss.

■ Example: Akbarbhai (80) is a milkman who has a shed, where he keeps 50 buffaloes of his own. Khan and two of his friends forcibly enter Akbarbhai's shed for a month threatening him with his life. All the milk collected in the month was sold by Khan and the proceeds were collected by him as well. In this situation, Khan is guilty of wrongful gain whereas Akbarbhai has suffered wrongful loss.

ACCIDENT

Any accident that occurs while performing a legal act with proper care and caution without any criminal intention or knowledge is not an offence.

RIGHT TO PRIVATE DEFENCE

Any act done in the exercise of private defense is not an offence. Every person has a right to defend himself, any other person and his property. However, in doing so the person should not be doing more than is necessary for the purposes of self defense.

■ Example: (1) Twelve-year-old Sunny is studying in the fifth standard. Every evening his father comes to pick him up from school. One evening when Sunny's father went to the school, he saw the school teacher hitting his son on the hands, with a wooden foot ruler. Unable to see this, he picked up an axe lying near by and hit the school teacher, injuring him seriously. Sunny's father will not be able to plead his case for private defense since he inflicted more harm than necessary.

■ Example (2) : If Sunny's father, had been insane and attempted to kill the school teacher, then he is not guilty of any offence BUT the school teacher will have the same right to self defence that he would have had, if Sunny's father was sane.

CRIMINAL CONSPIRACY

When two or more persons agree to perform an illegal act or a legal act by illegal means, it is said to be a criminal conspiracy. There must be two or more persons to constitute this offence since one person alone cannot conspire with himself.

HURT AND GRIEVOUS HURT

Whoever causes bodily pain, disease or infirmity to another, is said to cause hurt.

Hurt becomes grievous hurt when:
it results in permanent deprivation of the sight of either eye.
it results in permanent deprivation of the hearing of either ear.
it results in permanent disfiguration of head or face.
it results in fracture or dislocation of bone or tooth.

ASSAULT

When a person (A) makes a gesture knowing that such a gesture will cause anyone (let's say B) to apprehend that 'A' is about to use criminal force on 'B', he is said to commit an assault. Only words do not amount to assault.

■ Example : If A takes out a knife and walks threateningly towards B, A is said to commit assault.

KIDNAPPING

(1) Whoever takes a person <u>out of India</u> without his own consent or without the consent of some person who is authorized to consent on his behalf, he is said to kidnap that person. The person kidnapped in such a case may be a minor or an adult.

(2) Whoever, takes away a minor (male under 16 years or female under 18 years) or a person of unsound mind, without the consent of its guardian, is said to kidnap the minor or person from lawful guardianship.

ABDUCTION

When a person is compelled by force or by any deceitful means to move from any place, such person is said to be abducted. To attract the offence of abduction, the age of the person being abducted is not significant.

9

First Information Report (FIR)

It is rightly said, "If injustice is happening to your neighbour, you can sleep. Wait for your turn. You are next". What this implies is easy to understand- it appeals to us to do something.

As we are aware, crime rate is steadily on the rise, minute by minute. Not a single hour goes by without the television, radio and now the internet, not reporting a crime. Likewise not many newspapers or weeklies can report a crime free day.

It is our duty to inform the police and help them carry out investigation of the crime/s we may have witnessed. Some TV shows appeal to people encouraging them to help the police in tracing the criminals and bringing them to justice. Being an arm chair critic and blaming the police is not our only duty. We are responsible for our country as well.

The term First Information Report (FIR) implies giving the first information of a cognizable crime to the police. The information given to the officer-in-charge of a police station and recorded in writing by the officer as required under the law is known as First Information Report (FIR).

First Information Report (FIR)

Objective:

The main objective of the FIR is to ensure that that the police officer receives information at the earliest, to initiate investigation and ensure that the facts should not be forgotten or embellished.

Time of filing FIR

When a cognizable offence is committed, one should inform the police immediately by filing an FIR.

Who can file an FIR

An FIR can be filed by the complainant or an eye witness to the crime, or even a stranger.

Duty of Officer-in-Charge

Every bit of information relating to a crime, when given orally to the officer-in-charge of a police station, must be noted by him in writing and read out to the informant. The information should also be signed by the person giving it, and the core of the matter must be entered in the book which is to be kept by such officer. A copy of the information recorded is also given *free of cost* to the informant.

Refusal by Officer-in-Charge to record the information

If the officer-in-charge of the police station refuses to record such information, one can send the same by post to the Superintendent of Police.

Power of officer-in-charge to record the information outside his station limit

A station house officer has the power to receive the information and record the same even if it is outside his station limits.

It is to be remembered that the FIR forms the basis of the case. Whether it is true or false, it usually represents what case the informant intended to set up at that time. The following four points should be noted about an FIR:

- it should be a fact of information disclosing that a cognizable offence was committed.

- it should be definite enough to enable the police officer to start investigation. It must not be vague, making it impossible or rather difficult to initiate investigation.
- it may be given by anybody.
- it is necessary that the offender or the witnesses should be named.

■ Example : At 5.00 pm on Friday evening, on 10th August, 2003, Inspector Kulkarni got a call from an unknown person who said that he saw a man with a big suitcase in his hand moving towards Tony Max theatre where premiere show of the movie Hartaal was about to start. Around 5.30 pm he got another call, also from from unknown person who said that he saw a man with a big suitcase in his hand, meeting two persons outside the Tony Max theatre and also overheard them discussing something about a mission. He suspected that there could be bomb inside the bag and they might have a plan to carry out a blast inside the theatre.

The information which Inspector Kulkarni received at 5.00 pm was not the FIR. However, the subsequent call received around 5.30 pm, was in fact, the FIR which enabled the inspector to investigate the matter.

It is not necessary that any form of information given first in point of time is to be treated as the FIR. It is essential that the information must relate to the committing of a cognizable offence directly, and not merely on the basis of possible, future events.

■ Example : Raghavan made a statement to the police, stating that he had not seen his neighbour Ram since the past two days. After two days, in his second statemen, Raghavan stated that he had neither seen Ram nor his wife since the past four days. He also complained of a dirty stench emitting from Ram's house. Raghavan suspected that his neighbours might not be alive.

In this case, the statement made by Mr.Raghavan after four days is what really amounts to an FIR because it was this statement and not the previous one, which matters.

However, the following statements do not come within the purview of an FIR:

- a statement given to the police after the investigation has commenced.
- a statement made by a witness at the time of inquiry.
- a statement recorded by an officer-in-charge on the basis of his personal knowledge after the original information was received.

Punishment for giving false information to the police

A person who gives false information to the police is liable for punishment. Even if such information is not reduced to writing, he nevertheless can be accused for making a false charge under the IPC (Indian Penal Code).

An FIR adds tremendous *value* to a case. It serves as a base. It can be used for the purpose of testing the truth of the facts.

Therefore, it is duty of a police officer to record the FIR and enter the factss in the diary as they are stated or narrated to him. If the officer records and enters the information differently, he would be guilty.

10

Bail

One often comes across articles in newspapers and television news channels regarding bail applications being made, granted or refused but heavily contested. With the crime rate increasing day by day, the terms bail, anticipatory bail and the circumstances under which it can be granted or not granted, become relevant. Bail applications can be made in cases ranging from religious offences, accidental death, illegal dealings in foreign exchange to dowry harassment, dowry death, poaching etc.

BAILABLE OFFENCE

A bail is nothing but a security. A bailable offence simply means an offence for which bail can be granted. It may include - absconding to avoid service of court summons from a public servant, bribery in elections, defamation. etc., Bail may be given by the officer, in charge of a police station who has custody of the accused, or by the court. If the accused is not arrested for a non-bailable offence, unnecessary hindrances should not be placed in the way of his getting bail. More than one application can be made for bail.

NON-BAILABLE OFFENCE

When any person is accused or suspected of committing a non-bailable offence, he shall not be released if (1) it reasonably appears that he is guilty of an offence punishable with death or life imprisonment; (2) the offence is a cognizable offence and such person had been previously convicted of an offence punishable with death or life imprisonment.

Non-bailable offences include sedition, kidnapping with intent to murder, fraudulently trying to destroy or deface a will, etc.

COGNIZABLE AND NON-COGNIZABLE CASES

A cognizable case is one in which a police officer may arrest the person without a warrant. Such instances include rioting, sedition, harbouring an offender if the offence, involving capital or in the nature of robbery or dacoity.

A non-cognizable case is one where a police officer has no authority to arrest without a warrant. Such instances include absconding to avoid service of court summons from a public servant or escape from confinement where a public servant was negligent.

ANTICIPATORY BAIL

Any person believing that he may be arrested on an accusation of having committed a non-bailable offence, may apply to the proper court for bail. The court may, if it thinks fit, direct that the accused be released on bail.

When the court makes such a direction it may include certain conditions such as:

(i) the person will make himself available for interrogation by a police officer.
(ii) he shall not threathen any person familiar with the facts so as to deter him from disclosing facts.
(iii) he shall not leave India without prior permission.

This provision of law applies only to non-bailable offences of all kinds.

In such cases the court has to consider:

(1) seriousness of the offence: the court has to consider the nature and gravity of the offence.
(2) nature of the accusation: the facts leading to the accusation of the person suspected of committing the offence.

(3) antecedents of the applicant: including his past record. Whether the applicant has a previous criminal record is an important factor.

(4) possibility of leaving the country: if he is granted anticipatory bail, whether he is likely to flee the country.

(5) society: The person's social status in society. The court also has to consider whether granting bail will endanger safety of society, at large.

The court has to use its power to grant anticipatory bail in exceptional circumstances. However, the accused has to prove that his case falls under those exceptional circumstances.

■ Example : A person was accused of killing a protected species of wildlife. He applied for, and secured anticipatory bail. However, in this case it was mandatory for him to obtain the permission of the court, as and when he intended to travel abroad and the court had the right to refuse permission.

11
Defamation

When any person, by words either spoken or in writing or by signs, makes or publishes any imputation (allegation) concerning another person with the intention to harm that person or knowing that the imputation will harm the reputation of such person he is said to defame that person.

■ Example: Amrita had gone with a group of people to watch a movie. During the film Amrita asked Aniket whether he knew who had stolen her mobile phone since it was missing. Aniket said that Zahir had stolen it, knowing fully well that actually, he himself was the culprit.

In this case, even if Aniket did not have knowledge as to who had stolen the phone, but if he intentionally accused Zahir, Aniket would be liable for defamation.

Note : An imputation is said to harm a person's reputation when it directly or indirectly lowers the moral or intellectual character of that person or lowers the person in respect of his caste or otherwise. An imputation made towards a deceased person may amount to defamation if it were to harm the reputation of that person if living and is upsetting to his near and dear ones.

THE OFFENCE OF DEFAMATION

The offence of defamation requires:

1. an imputation to be made or published against any person.

2. the imputation to be in the form of words or signs or visible representations.
3. such imputation must be made with the intention of harming the person to whom it is directed.

The defamatory matter must be published that is it must be communicated to some other person other than to whom it is directed.

■ Example : (1) Mr. Bhargava sends a post card with defamatory matter written on it. (2) Mr. Saxena in a letter sent by registered post makes certain defamatory remarks.

Bhargava is liable while Saxena is not.

It is not necessary that the complaint should be filed by the person who is defamed. An imputation was made against a leading pharmaceutical company. The court permitted one of the company's directors to file a complaint on behalf of the company.

Instances

- Newspapers: the publisher of a newspaper is responsible for the defamatory matter that is published therein whether he is aware of the contents or not. In order to be charged for the offence of defamation, the owner of a tabloid must have a direct accountability for the publication of the defamatory matter along with the intention/knowledge that such publication will cause harm to another.

- Married Couple: false accusations made by the husband against his wife and spread in their housing society, stating that she is having an illicit affair with another person and that she is pregnant as a result of the same, fulfill the ingredients of defamation.

There are certain exceptions to defamation:

I. public benefit : an imputation concerning any person which is true does not amount to defamation if it is for the benefit of the public.

II. public servant : an opinion expressed in good faith concerning the conduct of a public servant (eg. police officer, minister) discharging his public functions.

III. fair reports : publishing of a substantially true report of the events in a Court of Justice.

■ Example : An article on a fraud case of the company Cragger's International Ltd., was published in The News. The article reported the decision of the court which heard and decided the case. This is not defamatory.

IV. caution : conveying of caution by one person to another for the latter's benefit.

V. conduct of witness : any opinion expressed in good faith regarding the conduct of any person as a party or as a witness as far as his character appears in that conduct alone is not defamation.

VI. censure : any criticism made by one person who has authority over another (either in law or by legal contract) in good faith, regarding the conduct of the other.

■ Example : Karim's father reprimanded him in the presence of other children since Karim did not go to school on time. There is no defamation.

VII. self protection : an allegation by a person with respect to the character of another for his own safety and protection.

■ Case: Mrs. Desai sent a legal notice to her husband through her lawyer claiming certain property. Mr. Desai's advocate replied to the notice through a letter containing insulting and defamatory matter. On a complaint made by Mrs. Desai for defamation, the court's dismissed the same, stating that communication to an advocate is not publication, in view of the relation between them. An advocate acts for and on behalf of his client and has no separate existence.

RELEVANT TERMS

- Libel – a publication (either in writing or in the form of pictures etc.), of a false and defamatory statement with an intention to harm the reputation of another person without legal explanation.

- Slander – false and defamatory words spoken or gestures made to harm the reputation of another.
- Innuendo – An explanation by the complainant defining the meaning which he assigns to the objectionable words, or stating that he is the person to whom the reference has been made.

■ Example: An Article was published in News hour stating that an all woman gang had kidnapped Anna, a minor girl. The article did not make any direct reference to the plaintiff. The plaintiff pleaded that it was common knowledge that she was part of an all woman group and also had close relations with Anna's family.

A suit restraining the publication of the defamatory material can be filed as a remedy for defamation. Damages can also be claimed.

Defences to an action for defamation include:

1. unintentional
2. bad reputation of the complainant.
3. tendering of apology at the earliest.
4. aggravation by the complainant.
5. absence of spite.

12

Offences Against The Government & Armed Forces

The first thought that comes to mind – are not the offences we have discussed before also offences against the government as such. Then why discuss them separately. The offences we are about to talk about are of a different nature, as you will see. These offences or crimes relate directly to the safety and protection of our very country. These are offences of a kind which threaten the peace of India.

- A reference to the government means and includes the State as well as the Union.

Let us see some of the offences which come under the category of:

OFFENCES OR CRIMES AGAINST THE GOVERNMENT

- *Waging a war* against the Government of India

    This is an offence punishable with death or life imprisonment and fine. Even an attempt or abetment to wage war is an offence. The attack on our Parliament by terrorists qualifies as an offence of this nature.

A conspiracy by certain persons to wage war against the Government also constitutes an offence.

Further, waging a war against an Asiatic Power which is an ally of the Government of India is an offence as well.

- Arms and Ammunition - whoever collects men, arms or ammunition or makes some other preparation to wage war against the Government shall also be punished.

- Assault against the Governor or the President - any assault or wrongful restraint over a Governor or the President with intention that such Governor or President is forced to exercise or refrain from exercising his lawful powers is an offence.

- Sedition – any person who by words, signs or otherwise brings feelings of enmity or attempts to do so towards the Government is liable to be punished for the offence of sedition.

- POW's (or Prisoners of War) – where a public servant having the custody of a State prisoner or a POW voluntarily allows such prisoner to escape, he shall be punished severely.

■ Example : The inspector of a police station in Bihar, had in his custody, a terrorist convicted of an attack on the minister of state. He helped the terrorist escape from his custody and also made his arrangements to travel outside the country. The officer is guilty.

OFFENCES AGAINST THE ARMED FORCES

- Any person who abets (assists) the committing of mutiny (revolt) by an officer of the Armed Forces shall be punished by the law. Such person shall also be punished when he attempts to seduce an officer from his allegiance (faithfulness) or his duty towards his country.

■ Example : Mr. Biharilal is a successful businessman operating from Central India. He has already been suspected to have links with hostile countries. Biharilal approached the Army Officer in his area for a favour. The favour being information of certain military codes. Biharilal is guilty of this offence.

Bearing the above offence in mind - where the person who abetted the committing of mutiny, will if mutiny is committed in consequence of the abetment, be punished even with death. In all cases the offence will have to be proved.

- Assault – similarly, when a person abets an assault by an officer against his superior acting in the execution of his duties he is liable to be punished.
- Desertion – abetment of desertion of any officer of the Army, Navy or the Air Force by any person is punishable. Harboring a 'deserter' when the person has knowledge or a reasonable doubt of the deserter being as such is a more severe offence.

However, when the captain or person in charge of a merchant ship proves that he was unaware of the deserter being on board his ship he can be let off lightly.

Part V
Law of Torts

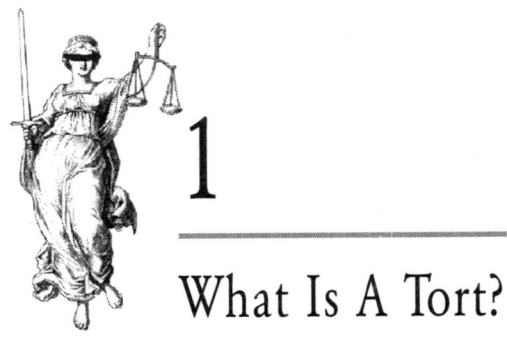

1

What Is A Tort?

A tort is a civil wrong. It is a breach of some duty which arises independently of a contract. The breach of such duty gives the victim or the person wronged, an opportunity to claim damages and compensation from the person who was to perform the duty.

■ Example : The Municipal Corporation of Indore has been carrying out road repairs every night. As a result, some parts of the roads have been dug. It is the duty of the corporation to ensure that there is sufficient warning for the motorists for their safety by installing "warning signs" and having proper lighting. One night Shrikant was driving down a road in his car, on which work was being carried out. He didn't see that the road was dug and fell inside. Consequently, he got hurt and suffered damages. Shrikant is entitled to compensation from the Corporation.

From this example it can be seen:

 (i) Shrikant is the victim who has suffered injury and damages;

 (ii) the Corporation is at fault for not ensuring the safety of motorists;

 (iii) although the Corporation did not expressly contract with Shrikant to ensure his safety, nevertheless it was its duty to ensure security and safety of the inhabitants of the city.

TORT AND CONTRACT

How is a tort distinguished from a contract?

In a tort, the duty is imposed by the law and is owed to the community at large. In the case of a contract, the duty is fixed by an agreement between the parties and affects only the parties to the contract.

■ Example of tort : Amar goes to Suresh's office and damages the office property without any reason. Suresh will be entitled to claim damages from Amar. The duty violated by Amar is imposed by the law i.e. not to cause harm to the person or property of another.

■ Example of contract : Akshay enters into an agreement with Superior Electronics for the supply of a colour television. The television supplied is defective. This is a breach of a specific duty by the supplier and therefore, Akshay is entitled to claim damages from them.

Wrongful Act

To constitute a tort, the act complained of, must be wrongful. That is it must be without a legal reason or excuse. Such wrongful act must have resulted in damages/injury to the complainant.

The word act also includes *omission* or *neglect* to do a particular act. Where it was the duty of the person/authority to do a particular act or to refrain from doing so and the person/authority so fails in its duty, in that event, the party having suffered damages can claim compensation from the person/authority.

Railway Crossing : At a railway crossing, it is the duty of the rail authorities to warn people when the train is approaching as well as informing them the correct time to cross the railway lines.

Does an action in tort arise when, although there was a breach of duty but no actual damage was suffered by the complainant?

Yes. An action in tort will arise in such a situation.

■ Example : A customer had sufficient balance in his savings account. However, the banker refused to clear one of his cheques. The banker is liable to the customer although he did not suffer any actual loss or damage by the act of the banker.

2

Nuisance

In our daily life, we often face problems such as pollution due to oil or poisonous gases, noise, air and water pollution from industries etc. All these are the causes of nuisance which cause us inconvenience.

Every individual has a right to live. This right also includes the right to live a peaceful and healthy life. This is a fundamental right given to us by our constitution. The law makes provisions to protect the same.

MEANING

The dictionary defines Nuisance as annoyance. It is an act done or an illegal omission resulting in injury or danger to an individual or to the society.

PROOF

(a) There must be some wrongful act done or illegal omission on part of the person, *and*

(b) The act or illegal omission results in injury, danger, damages or annoyance to any individual or the public at large.

CATEGORIES

Public Nuisance

Public Nuisance is an act or illegal omission which results in any common injury, danger or annoyance to the public or to the people in general, who reside or occupy property in the vicinity. The acts not only include acts which interfere with the definite public rights such as right of way, but also acts which cause general danger to the health, safety or comfort of the public.

Example :

(a) Escape of noxious gases and smokes from chimneys of factories
(b) Use of firecrackers etc.

Acts Under Legal Authority

No action will lie in cases where damage is caused by acts performed under legal authority. For instance, road concretization by the municipality which may result in noise pollution etc.

However, an action is maintainable in such cases, when more than necessary harm is caused while carrying the authorized act.

Also, a private individual cannot sue on account of public nuisance. In such a case, the individual has to prove special damages caused to him i.e. he has suffered specific injury or damages, beyond what have been suffered by the common public.

Private Nuisance

Private nuisance emanates from unauthorized use of one's property, causing damages or injury to the owner or occupier of the property. It includes material interference with the health or comfort of such person, but not amounting to trespass.

Examples :

Obstruction to air and light, escape of water, encroachment on neighbour's land.

■ For instance : Ajith is staying on the second floor of ABC building. Since the day he bought that flat, he is enjoying sunlight and air. Dixon Advertising firm, puts its neon signs in front of the windows of Ajith's flat obstructing air and light. Ajith is entitled to maintain an action against the obstruction caused by Dixon Advertising firm.

Persons entitled to sue

In cases of private nuisance, the actual occupier or owner can file a suit. If the property is occupied by tenants, the landlord can maintain a suit only if the damage done is continuing and of permanent nature. Only the person who has interest in the property or right to occupation is entitled to maintain the suit.

In cases of public nuisance, an advocate general or collector can maintain a suit.

3

Trespass To Goods

The word trespass means intrusion or encroachment. Trespass to goods is an unlawful disturbance of the possession of goods. It may be by seizure or removal and includes causing damage to the goods.

POSSESSION

The complainant must be in possession of the goods. A person who is in possession of the goods has a legal right against every third party with respect to the goods. Even deflating a car tyre amounts to trespass.

A trespasser cannot become the owner of the property. The owner is entitled to take back the property from the trespasser.

■ Example : Ravi, a farmer was the owner of cattle. His cattle would graze in his fields and would return home in the evening. One cow however, strayed into the neighbouring field. Amar, the farmer to whom the other field belonged thought it was his own cow and took her into the shed. Amar is entitled to defend a complaint made by Ravi on the ground that he thought the cow belonged to him.

However, Amar cannot say that he intentionally kept the cow with him since it had strayed on to his field, as long as the cow retained an intention to go back to her own field.

Killing or injuring an animal is also a form of trespass.

Proof: the complainant in his action for trespass must prove that:

(a) he was in possession of the goods.

(b) there is an illegal interference in his possession.

Defence to an action of trespass

(i) Self defence: where possession of a person (A) who is entitled to his property is wrongfully taken away by another (B), he (i.e. A) is justified in using the necessary force to prevent him (B) from doing so.

(ii) Complainant's own fault: for instance, the complainant parks his two-wheeler in the middle of the street and goes to purchase groceries. This obstructs the right of way. The two-wheeler can be removed by applying the necessary force for it.

CONVERSION

This takes place when one person intentionally interferes with any goods belonging to another, thereby depriving him of the use and possession of it. It includes destruction of goods.

Methods of conversion:

(i) by selling the goods.

(ii) taking them.

(iii) wrongfully parting with them.

Instances of conversion with examples:

■ wrongful selling of property : Ajith approaches a jeweller with a gold ring telling him that he should sell the ring for the best price, but not below Rs. 10,000/- The jeweller sells the ring for Rs. 5,000/- without informing Ajith and hands over the money to him.

■ wrongful acquisition of property : Evergreen Society consists of plots of land where individuals construct bungalows for themselves. Each such plot has a bungalow and rows of different kinds of trees. Some of these trees bearing fruit tend to hang into the land/plot belonging to the neighbouring plot owner. If the neighbouring plot owner collects the fruit from his neighbour's trees and uses them for himself, he is liable for conversion.

■ wrongful parting of property: Jindal handed over a parcel of goods to ABC Courier Company for having them delivered to his partner in Delhi. The courier company hands over the goods to another so as to give that other, some right over the property. The courier company commits conversion.

4
Negligence

We live in a civilized society and owe responsibility towards others. We are responsible for our acts and therefore should not harm anyone by our action or inaction.

It is our duty to respect the freedom of the other person. The Law has also recognized this duty and imposed a liability on the person who, by his act or omission has caused damages to another.

For instance, when a person drives his vehicle on the express highway, he is at liberty to drive faster, (within speed limit) as compared to when he is driving on a busy road where it is his duty to drive slower and watchfully, for the safety of pedestrians and other traffic.

MEANING

Negligence is a violation of duty. It is caused by failure to do such acts which in regular conduct of human affairs, a rational man will do.

NEGLIGENCE INCLUDES

the acts which a careful and reasonable man will not do. It also includes those acts which take place when a person does not use ordinary care or skill which is expected of him resulting in injury to a person or property of another.

Negligence

In this context, it must be noted:

- there must be the *existence* of a legal duty on the part of one person towards another.
- There must be a *failure* to perform such duty
- Consequential *damages* must be caused to another person.

■ Example : Ram bought chocolates of Mango India Pvt. Ltd. for his sons Ajay and Vijay. After eating half a chocolate bar, his sons found some dead worms inside it. They contracted a stomach infection.

It is the duty of Mango India Pvt. Ltd. to ensure that its products (chocolates) are fit for human consumption. The company failed to perform its duty towards its customers and is therefore liable.

In the case of negligence, the victim of the negligence should prove the following points :

(i) there was a legal obligation on the part of the person who caused the damages.

(ii) there was a failure to perform that duty or in exercising due care of skills

(iii) such duty was towards him.

It must be noted that :

- the damage caused was the actual result of non-performance of the duty.
- there is a direct connection between damage and negligence on part of the person who caused the damages.

■ Example: Pravin was walking along the roadside in the night. Municipal workers had dug a ditch for repair work. Neither had the authorities covered it properly nor was there any warning sign in place. Pravin, who was unaware of the ditch due to the dark, could not see it. He fell in it and sustained considerable injuries. The municipality is liable to pay damages to Pravin.

In this case, it was the duty of the municipal workers to cover the ditch properly or place warning signs. However, the municipality failed to perform its duty towards the public.

In the following cases, the person who caused damages to another person due to negligence is *not liable* to compensate another person.

Acts of God : the acts that happen as a result of elementary forces of nature (for example - storm, lightning, flood, extraordinary high tide etc.) are known as Acts of God. These acts cannot be foreseen and are beyond the control of any human being.

■ Example : Ajay and Vijay were walking on the road when it started pouring. They took shelter under a shop. Suddenly one tree which was a part of an adjoining bungalow fell on the roof of the shop injuring Vijay. Vijay cannot claim compensation from the bungalow owner as the accident happened due to heavy rain.

Contributory Negligence : this is when the victim himself has contributed to his situation. It results from negligence which is partly due to negligence of the person who suffered loss and damages. If such person had acted diligently, he could have avoided the consequences of the negligence of the other person.

■ Example : If a person hangs dangerously at the doors of a railway compartment and falls, thereby sustains injuries, the railway administration is not liable because the person who hangs as such, is knowingly exposing himself to risks.

Note (1) : Negligence on the part of children : children of tender age cannot judge the consequences of their acts and therefore cannot be held liable. Also, children cannot be expected to act reasonably or with caution.

■ Example : Raj left his key in the car and went into shop. Eight-year-old Rajeev who was near the car, opened the door and sat inside. Suddenly, Rajeev started the car and dashed it against the wall injuring himself and damaging the car.

Rajeev cannot be expected to act diligently as Raj was negligent by not properly locking his car and also leaving the key in . Raj is liable to compensate Rajeev.

Note (2) : Alternative Danger: when the person who suffered loss and damage is placed in such a situation due to which he chooses the dangerous way of escape and thereby suffers, the person who caused the damages is liable to compensate.

Negligence

■ Example : When Sajid was crossing the road, he saw a speeding car coming towards him and ran. Unfortunately, a truck from the opposite direction hit him and he was injured. The car driver is liable to pay Sajid.

Unavoidable Accidents

Accidents take place in every part of the world. Under this category, the rule of negligence is not applicable.

■ Example : Viren was driving on the highway. He saw a speeding truck coming towards him from the opposite direction and to avoid being hit he diverted his car. Unfortunately, he hit a mechanic who was repairing a car along the roadside. This is a case of inevitable accident, therefore Viren is not liable.

5

Master & Servant Relation

This chapter describes the circumstances where the master is liable for the acts committed by his servant and the consequences of the same. Every person is liable for his own acts and not for those committed by others. However, in certain cases, the liability extends to the acts committed by another as well. This is called Vicarious Liability.

A *servant* is a person who obeys the lawful orders and directions of another in respect of certain work to be done, whether for salary/wages or without it.

A *master* is a person capable of giving the orders and directions and who ensures that they are properly followed. A son is not a servant of the father.

■ Example: Ajay sent his car to the garage, for repairs. The car was stolen and subsequently, recovered at the scene of crime. Ajay is not liable, in this case. Once the car is handed over to the garage it becomes the responsibility of the garage owner to look after it.

Generally, a master is liable for the acts of his servant because he himself is unable to do them, either:

(a) due to paucity of time, or
(b) age/ill-health, or
(c) if the work involves a specific skill etc.

Master & Servant Relation

Therefore, the master is responsible for all acts done by a servant in the course of service, and which are said to have the master's express or implied authority for the same.

TYPES OF LIABILITIES

A. Master's liability to a servant.

It is the duty of a master to:

(i) provide competent co-workers to his servants.

(ii) provide a healthy working atmosphere, proper tools and ensure that they are maintained in good condition;

(iii) be concerned regarding the safety of his servants.

Common Employment: a master is not liable where damage/injury has been suffered by one servant on account of another co-servant, under one employment and having one master.

■ Example : Tasty Chips is a factory which makes potato chips. The workers work in two shifts. It is the duty of the workers of the morning shift to ensure that the machines are working smoothly, and that no equipment is out of place, for the benefit of the night shift. However, no one noticed that some cutting devices were not in line with the others and as a result when the machine started the blades cut the hand of the factory worker managing the post. The master is not liable for the injuries caused to the co-worker.

- A servant is liable for his acts to the master when the servant has committed a wrongful act or has been negligent in committing an act during the course of employment with his master.

B. Liability of a master to third persons for the acts of a servant.

Three things that make the master liable are:

(i) the act must be committed by the servant in the course of his employment with the master.

(ii) the servant has committed a wrongful act.

(iii) the servant has done an act on the orders of the master but has done it wrongfully.

- The master is not responsible to any person when the act complained of has been done by the servant outside the scope of his employment with the master.

Delegation of authority by a servant of the master

The liability of the master, when a servant delegates his authority to another, depends upon the circumstances of the case and whether the servant has the authority of the master to delegate his duties.

OTHER RELATIONSHIPS

A. Company and its Directors

Companies are liable for the wrongful acts committed by their directors during the course of employment. The acts should be done in the interest of the company. The company will not be held responsible for the acts done by its directors in their personal capacity although they may be for the benefit of the company.

B. A Partnership Firm and its Partners

Each partner is liable to third parties for acts which are committed by their co-partners in the course of their partnership. A partner will not be able to deny his liability on the ground that he was unaware of the liability incurred by the other partner.

6

Trespass Of Immoveable Property

Trespass is any act which involves an unjustifiable entry upon the land of one person (B) by another (A). It is an invasion of one person's property by another.

CHARACTERISTICS

1. Entry: To constitute the offence of trespass there must be an *entry* upon the land of one person by another.
2. Unlawful: Such entry must be *unjustifiable or unlawful* i.e. without the permission of the person to whom the land belongs.

■ Example: Biharilal is a farmer by occupation. He has his own facilities in so far as water, oxen, fertilizers etc. are concerned. Banwarilal, a farmer in the neighbouring land does not have the benefit of these facilities. When Biharilal is unaware, he enters the land and makes use of the water facilities belonging to Biharilal and also diverts some of the water supply to his land. Banwarilal is guilty of trespass.

AUTHORITY OF LAW

A person entering into the property of another is a trespasser when he abuses the authority under which he enters the property.

■ Example : Avinash and friends go to a cinema hall. They buy the movie tickets and take their seats. In the course of the movie, Avinash shouts obscenities, tampers with the furniture and causes disturbance to the people around him. Hence, he loses the implied authority of the law and may be forced to leave the hall.

LICENSE

Under a leave and license agreement, the person who gives the property on license, is the licensor. The person accepting the license is the licensee. The licensee only has the permission for use of the flat by the licensor and the entire possession, right and title remains with the licensor. The licensee cannot do anything contrary to the terms of the agreement. If he does so, the license comes to an end as per the terms of the agreement between the parties and from that day onwards, the licensee becomes a trespasser.

EASEMENTS

Every person having ownership of land also has certain rights incidental to the land such as right to water, support, right of way etc.

Any unwarranted interference in respect to such rights amounts to action under the above provision.

Examples

■ Right of Way: Abhay was residing in a plot owners' society. The entry to his plot was through the common road shared between his plot and his neighbour Akhil. Construction of an out house by Akhil on the common road resulted in Abhay's path being blocked. Akhil is liable to Abhay.

■ Water: in a certain village, agricultural plots were irrigated by a stream which flowed from the nearby hills. An agricultural plot that belonged to Ramniklal received water from the stream before it went to Hazarilal. Ramniklal is under a duty to use the stream water properly. He cannot pollute the water and make it unfit for agricultural use by the other farmers in the village.

CHANGE OF USER OF THE LAND

A person who is in possession of property with the permission of the owner, either under a lease or otherwise, is not entitled to change the nature of usage of the land. If the land was leased for agricultural purposes, he cannot make commercial use of the land.

When such change of user takes place without the permission of the land owner, the relationship comes to an end and the lessee has to handover the property back to the lessor.

DEFENCES TO AN ACTION OF TRESSPASS

The defendant (person against whom a complaint has been made or action taken) can raise the following defences to the action:

1. Public Good : the defendant can succeed if he proves that the act complained of, was actually for public good or public safety.

2. Legally Entitled : if he can prove that he was allowed to enter the land or continue to remain on the land under legal authority.

3. By Contract : if according to him, the lease is continuing and he is observing the conditions of the same.

4. Protection : where he proves that he had no choice but to cause damage or trespass for his own self protection or that of his family members or of things belonging to him. However, the defendant will be liable when it is proved that he had done more harm than was necessary to protect himself.

7

Libel Slander & Innuendo

Libel is a form of defamation. Defamation has been discussed earlier.

LIBEL

A libel is a publication of a false and defamatory statement. Such statement must be made with the intention of injuring or harming the reputation of another person.

Contents :

1. In writing: the statement must be in some permanent form. That is, written or printed (newspapers, magazines). It may even be exhibited on audio or visuals, such as by means of a cinema film.

2. Intention: the statement must be made with the intention to harm the reputation of another person.

3. False: the statement must be false. Making of a true statement cannot amount to libel.

4. Without reason: the statement is made without any reason or excuse.

■ Example: Sheela was a leading film actress. She had acted in a few hit films earlier. Articles were published in magazines and newspapers suggesting that she obliged her directors to get roles for herself. Photographs were published where she was shown in a compromising position. In actual fact, this was not true. The editors of the publications were guilty of libel.

SLANDER

This too is a false and defamatory statement.

Requirements of slander:

1. it must be defamatory.
2. it must be false and made without any reason whatsoever.

Innuendo: when a statement is not defamatory on the face of it, but it may nevertheless, convey a defamatory meaning depending on the circumstances in which it is used. In other words, although the intention is there to say something defamatory it is not supported in those many words.

■ Example : A statement that Alan is a very good boy, however, one has to be careful when lending him money, is an innuendo.

8

Strict Liability

The law imposes strict liability on a person who has such things in his possession which are, by their nature, very dangerous to the life of a person or property. Under this rule persons are liable although they are not at fault.

(A) WHEN SIMPLE THINGS BECOME DANGEROUS

Anything (viz. water, motor car, electricity, filth etc.) which, if brought by a person ('A') for his own purpose in his premises, escapes and causes damage to another person ('B'), the one ('A') who keeps such things is answerable to the other ('B'). The law imposes absolute liability despite the fact that (i) At the time of keeping such things the person was not aware of the danger. (ii) And even if he was not owner of that premises.

However, there are certain exceptions to this rule. These are instances where 'A' will have a valid defence. Such as:

- *Act of God*: it includes the acts which are caused by the elementary forces of nature. Example- storms, lightning, extraordinary fall of rain, extraordinary high tide etc.
- *Own Default*: where the damage is due to the person's (suffering the loss) own fault, no action will lie.
- *Public Purpose*: any thing lawfully done for a public purpose in discharge of a public duty without negligence is excepted.

Strict Liability

- *Common Benefit*: when some work is done for the common benefit of (A) and (B) and if by accident (A) suffered loss, (B) is not liable to (A) or When work is done with (A)'s consent B is not liable.

(B) DANGEROUS GOODS

The person who is dealing in goods or using such goods for his own purpose which, are by their nature, very dangerous to human life (Explosives, fire arms, poisonous drugs, gas, machinery) is bound to take utmost care.

The Bhopal gas leak tragedy is a leading case in point.

■ Example : Ajay is dealing in petrol. He keeps petrol cans in his godown adjoining Shyam's house. A fire breaks out in the godown and spreads to Shyam's house. The house is destroyed and Shyam also suffers physical injuries. Shyam is entitled to compensation from Ajay.

DANGEROUS ANIMALS

The person who keeps animals who, by their nature are dangerous (Lion, bear, crocodile etc) does so at his own risk. With domestic animals such as cat, dog etc, the responsibility is less, although the keeper of the animal is under obligation to keep it under control and ensure that no harm is caused to another person.

OCCUPIERS OF PREMISES

The occupier of a premise is under obligation to warn other persons entering the premises of the dangers of the premise, if any –

(a) As of right : when person enters the premise as of right, for instance, postman, policemen etc., the premise should be made safe for them. They should be informed of danger, if any, in the premises.

(b) By invitation : when a person enters the premise as an invitee of the occupier classified as:

 (i) By express invitation: when a person enters the premise on an express invitation, such as a guest, the occupier must warn him of any dangers of which he is aware

(ii) By implied invitation: when the person enters into the premise on an implied invitation, the occupier is under obligation to inform him of any possible dangers. For instance, customers at a shop, patients in hospital.

(c) Person entering without permission : a person who enters in the premises of another person without permission or consent of that person or without any right to enter is a Trespasser. If any harm is caused to the trespasser, the occupier is not liable.

Example: Ajay entered Raj Malhotra's house to ask for an address When he was bitten by Malhotra's dog. Malhotra is not liable to Ajay as Ajay had no right to enter the premises without Malhotra's permission..

(d) Licensee : a licensee is a person who enters into the premises of the occupier under a license. It is duty of the occupier to caution him against any known risks or hazards of which he is aware but the licensee is ignorant.

Example : Amit permitted Nimit to enter his garden. There was one hole in the garden which was usually covered with sand. One evening, Amit's dog uncovered it, as a result of which, Nimit fell into the hole and sustained injuries. Amit is liable to pay damages to Nimit.

(e) Public : when a person is lawfully passing by the premises of another, it is the duty of the occupier to guard that person against any risks or dangers of which he is aware.

(f) Talented persons : persons who possess special skills and knowledge are under obligation to act diligently and in a skillful manner. Following are the persons from whom this is expected.

(i) Directors : Directors of a public limited company who handle the business of the company are responsible for its survival. Therefore they are accountable for the money entrusted to them by the public.

(ii) Carriers of Goods : the duty of a carrier of the goods is that of an insurer. He should take utmost care from the day he receives the goods till its delivery. He is answerable for loss and damages to goods even if he is not at fault.

(iii) Carriers of Passengers : a carrier is under obligation to make the journey of its passengers safe, by taking proper care and providing all necessary facilities.

(iv) Hotels : these are responsible for the safety of the luggage of guests which they are entrusted with and are liable if the same are stolen.

(v) Surgeons : utmost care is expected of persons who enter into a learned profession. Among these, physicians and surgeons are required to act fairly, diligently and to employ competent degrees of skill.

(vi) Solicitors : a solicitor is expected to be prudent in the application of his knowledge and should he diligent in matters entrusted to him by his client.

(vii) Bankers : they are responsible for the money entrusted to them by their customers. If any wrong payment is made on account of a forged signature, the bank will be liable to compensate its customer.

Part VI

Constitution of India

1
Citizenship

A citizen is a person who is a member of a nation. He enjoys the privileges and freedom given by the country, as distinguished from a foreigner. A citizen can only be a natural person. Although corporations may be nationals of the country for the purposes of international law, they are not citizens.

CITIZENSHIP : Is the status of being a citizen. The right is a national right. It depends neither on the sex of the individual nor his age.

DOMICILE : Is the place where a man has his home. It is the place where one has the permanent intention of returning to.

Every person has his domicile in the territory of India:

(a) who was born in the territory of India; *or*
(b) either of whose parents was born in the territory of India; *or*
(c) who has been residing in India for not less than five years immediately preceding the commencement of the Constitution of India. (i.e. January 26, 1950).

   (1) To be a citizen of India, it is most important that a person has an Indian domicile.
   (2) He may himself be born in India or either of his parents may be born in India.
   (3) A person may be citizen of India irrespective of the nationality of his parents.

MIGRANTS TO INDIA FROM PAKISTAN

A person who has migrated to India from the territory now of Pakistan, is a citizen of India if :

(a) he or either of his parents or grandparents was born in India; *and*

(b) he has migrated to India before July 19, 1948 and has been residing in India since the date of his migration.

MIGRANTS TO PAKISTAN FROM INDIA

A person who has migrated from India to Pakistan after March 1, 1947, is not a citizen of India. However, if he, after having migrated, returns to India under a permit of resettlement or permanent return he will be treated as though he had migrated after July 19, 1948.

A person who visits Pakistan temporarily for some business purpose or otherwise, would not lose his Indian citizenship.

CITIZENSHIP OF ANOTHER COUNTRY

Where a person voluntarily acquires the citizenship of another state/country, he loses his citizenship of India.

Instances how a person can become a citizen of India under the Indian Citizenship Act, 1955.

- By Birth : every person born in India on or after January 26, 1950 becomes a citizen of India by birth.
- By Descent : a person who is born outside India on or after January 26, 1950 becomes a citizen of India if his father is a citizen of India at the time of his birth.
- Registration : the proper authority may register a person as a citizen of India if the person makes an application:
    (a) that he is of Indian origin and has been residing in India for six months preceding the date of his application.
    (b) that she is a woman who is married to a citizen of India.
    (c) that he is a minor child of a person who is a citizen of India.

2

Right To Freedom

The right to freedom of a citizen includes the right to :
(1) freedom of speech and expression.
(2) assemble (gather) peaceably and without arms.
(3) form associations and unions.
(4) move freely throughout the territory of India.
(5) practice any profession.

1. The Freedom of speech and expression

This means the right to express one's convictions freely either in words - spoken or in writing, in print, by pictures, by electronic device or otherwise. The freedom of speech and expression also includes freedom of the press and extends to exhibiting of advertisements, cinematographic films etc.

Restrictions : This freedom is restricted, for instance where the security of the State is threatened or when it causes defamation to a person.

2. Freedom to assemble

Citizens are allowed to assemble peaceably and without arms and ammunition. Citizens are allowed to hold meetings in large numbers provided they are held peacefully and without arms and ammunition.

3. Freedom to form associations and unions

Citizens have the right to form associations and unions. However, this right is subject to the power of the state to impose any reasonable restrictions on such rights.

We find *morchas* (processions) etc. being taken out by people who have certain grievances (for instance) against the government. The carrying out of these *morchas* is subject to the restrictions imposed by the state in this regard.

4. Freedom to move freely throughout India

This freedom is necessary so that citizens are able to transcend their states and experience and reside in another state of their choice.

■ Example : A resident of Maharashtra can move (transfer) to a state of his choice, for instance, Tamil Nadu. He has the right to reside and settle in any part of the country.

5. Freedom to practice any profession

Every citizen has a right to practice any profession or to carry on any occupation, trade or business of his choice. The state may impose certain restrictions in respect to the practice of any profession or in carrying on any occupation, trade or business.

■ Example : To practice as a lawyer, the state requires a person to pass his LLB examination.

The right to carry on business includes the right to close the business as well.

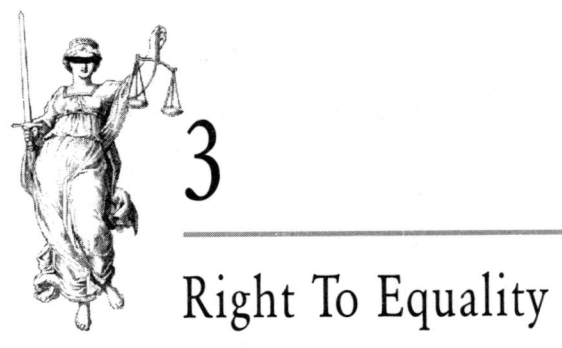

3

Right To Equality

Every person has a right to be treated equally and without discrimination.

RIGHT TO EQUALITY INCLUDES :

(1) the right to equality before the law.

(2) no discrimination only on the grounds of religion, race, caste, sex or place of birth.

(3) equal opportunities in public employment.

(4) abolition of untouchability.

(5) abolition of titles.

1. Equality before the law and equal protection of the law.

No person must be denied equality before the law or equal protection by the law. Equality before the law means the absence of any special privilege in favour of any particular person before the law. The law should treat all persons alike and without discrimination.

However, this does not apply in all cases, for example:

(i) land owners and tenants.

(ii) citizens and non-citizens etc.

2. No discrimination on the grounds of religion, race, caste, sex or place of birth.

No citizen will be discriminated against only on the grounds of religion, sex, caste, race, place of birth.

Further, no citizen will on any of these above grounds face any restriction with regard to :

(a) access to shops, public restaurants, hotels and places of public entertainment;

(b) the use of wells, tanks, bathing ghats etc. that are maintained out of state funds and are dedicated to the use of the general public.

- The state may make special provisions for women and children under this category.

For example: free education for children.

3. Equal opportunity in public employment

There will be equality of opportunity for all citizens in matters relating to employment or appointment to any public office. No citizen is to be discriminated against or be ineligible for employment under any office of the state only on the grounds of religion, sex, caste, race, place of birth.

Backward classes: the state may provide for reservation of posts in favour of any backward classes of citizens, who according to the state are not adequately represented.

4. Abolition of untouchability

Untouchability is a social disability imposed on certain classes of persons due to their birth in certain castes. Untouchability is abolished and its practice in any form is forbidden.

Offence : any person wanting to put into effect any disability of another arising out of untouchability, is guilty of an offence punishable by law.

For instance, where a particular person is prevented from entering any religious place because he is an 'untouchable'. In such a situation, the authorities or persons instrumental in preventing such a person from entering a religious place are guilty of an offence and are liable to be punished.

5. Abolition of titles

No titles will be given by the state unless it is a military or academic title. The conferring of titles which was once in practice has subsequently been abolished.

Acceptance of title from a foreign state:

(i) no citizen of India will accept a title from a foreign state.
(ii) no person who is not a citizen of India (while he is holding an office under the state) will accept any title from any foreign state without the consent of the President of India.

4

Fundamental Duties

The Constitution of India lays down the fundamental duties to be observed by every citizen of India. These include :

- to abide by the Constitution and respect the National flag and the National anthem.
- to uphold and protect the sovereignty (dominion), unity and integrity (honour) of India.
- to promote harmony and the spirit of common brotherhood transcending religious, regional or sectional diversities.
- to renounce practices that are derogatory to women.
- to protect and improve our natural environment such as forests, lakes, rivers etc.
- to safeguard public property.
- to defend the country and render national service when called upon to do so.
- to preserve the rich heritage of our culture.
- to cherish and follow the noble ideals which inspired our struggle to the freedom of India.

The fundamental duties of citizens cannot be *enforced.*

5

The Parliament (Union Legislature)

CONSTITUTION

The Parliament consists of the President of India and two Houses known as the Council of States and the House of the People.

A. THE COUNCIL OF STATES (THE RAJYA SABHA)

Composition

The Rajya Sabha consists of 12 members to be nominated by the President, having special knowledge or experience in literature, science, art and social service *and*

Not more than 238 representatives of the states and union territories.

Election

The representatives of each State are to be elected by the elected Members of the Legislative Assembly of the state.

Duration

The Council of States is not subject to dissolution. However, 1/3rd of the members retire on the expiration of every second year.

Qualifications

A person qualifies to be a Member of the Rajya Sabha, if:

1. he is a citizen of India.
2. he is not less than 30 years of age *and*
3. he possesses such other qualifications as the Parliament may prescribe.

Chairman and Deputy Chairman

The Vice President of India will be the *ex-officio* Chairman. The Council will choose a member to be Deputy Chairman.

B. THE HOUSE OF THE PEOPLE (THE LOK SABHA)

Composition

The Lok Sabha consists of not more than 530 Members who are directly elected by the people *and* not more than 20 Members to represent the Union Territories as the Parliament may provide.

Each state is allotted a number of seats in the Lok Sabha in such a manner that the number and the population of the state, is the same for all states. Further, each State is divided into territorial constituencies in such a manner that the ratio between the population of each constituency and the number of seats allotted to it, remains the same throughout the State.

Duration

The Lok Sabha will continue for five years from the date of its first meeting, unless it is dissolved earlier.

Qualifications

A person qualifies to be a member of the Lok Sabha if :

1. he is a citizen of India.
2. he is not less than 25 years of age *and*
3. he possesses such other qualifications as the Parliament may prescribe.

Speaker and Deputy Speaker

The Lok Sabha will choose two Members of the House to be Speaker and Deputy Speaker.

DISQUALIFICATION OF MEMBERS

A person will be disqualified from being a Member of either House of Parliament for any of the following reasons:

(i) he holds an office of profit under the state or central government, unless the Parliament declares otherwise.

(ii) he is of unsound mind and is declared by the court as such.

(iii) he is not a citizen of India.

(iv) he is an undischarged insolvent.

- No person can be a Member of both Houses of Parliament. So also, no person can be both, a Member of the House of Parliament and the House of Legislature of the state.

POWERS AND PRIVILEGES OF MEMBERS

1. Every Member will have freedom of speech in Parliament.
2. No Member of Parliament is liable to any court proceeding in respect of anything said, or any vote given by him in Parliament.
3. Members are also entitled to receive salaries and allowances as may be determined from time to time by the Parliament.

6

State Legislature

Every State has a legislature provided under the Constitution of India.

(i) In the States of Bihar, Maharashtra, Karnataka and Uttar Pradesh there are two Houses namely *Legislative Council* and *Legislative Assembly and the Governor.*

(ii) In other states, there is one House known as the *Legislative Assembly and the Governor.*

However, the Parliament has the authority to 'abolish' a Legislative Council of states having a Legislative Council. It also has the right to 'create' a Legislative Council where States do not have one.

LEGISLATIVE ASSEMBLY

Composition

The Legislative Assembly for each State will consist of a minimum of 60 members and a maximum of 500 members. The members are chosen by direct election from territorial constituencies in the state.

Duration

The Legislative Assembly of every State will continue for *five years* unless it is dissolved earlier.

Qualifications

To qualify for a seat in the Legislative Assembly, a person must be:

(a) a citizen of India *and*

(b) not less than 25 years of age.

Officers

Every Legislative Assembly of the state must have a speaker and a deputy speaker.

LEGISLATIVE COUNCIL

Composition

The total number of members in the Legislative Council of a state (having such a council) shall not exceed $1/3^{rd}$ of the total number of members in the Legislative Assembly of that state. The total number however, must not be less than 40.

Duration

The Legislative Council of a state is not subject to dissolution. However, almost $1/3^{rd}$ of its members retire after every two years.

Qualifications

To qualify for a seat in the Legislative Council, a person must be:

(a) a citizen of India *and*

(b) not less than 30 years of age.

Officers

The Legislative Council of every state which has a Legislative Council, will choose two members from it to be chairman and deputy chairman.

VOTING

All questions, when a House of Legislature is in progress are to be determined by a majority of votes of the members present, other than the Speaker (Legislative Assembly) or the Chairman (in the case of a Legislative Council).

DISQUALIFICATIONS FOR MEMBERSHIP

A person will be disqualified from being a member of the Legislative Assembly or Legislative Council of a State if :

(i) he holds an office of profit under the state or central government unless the Parliament declares otherwise.

(ii) he is of unsound mind and is declared by the court as such.

(iii) he is not a citizen of India.

(iv) he is an undischarged insolvent.

7

Emergency

The word Emergency suggests imminent danger or sudden danger or danger that requires action.

WHO CAN MAKE A PROCLAMATION OF EMERGENCY

The President of India can proclaim an emergency in certain situations to take effect in the *whole* or *part* of India.

CIRCUMSTANCES FOR PROCLAMATION OF EMERGENCY

A. SECURITY OR SAFETY OF INDIA

If the President of India is satisfied that grave emergency exists whereby the security or safety of India or any part of India is threatened by war or external aggression or armed rebellion.

For instance: A proclamation of emergency was issued by the President of India in October, 1962 at the time of the Chinese invasion.

Revocation of a Proclamation

A proclamation of emergency may be *revoked* by a subsequent proclamation.

Effects of Proclamation of Emergency

During the subsistence of an emergency there are certain restrictions on the rights of the citizens of the country. These include :

1. Suspension of enforcement of fundamental rights

During an emergency, the President of India may suspend the right to approach any court for the enforcement of fundamental rights as provided under the Constitution of India and also suspend the right to continue such proceedings when they have been started.

2. Suspension of rights such as freedom of speech, to move freely throughout India, to practice any profession etc.

While a proclamation of an emergency is in operation, rights such as freedom of speech and expression and freedom of the press may be suspended. So also, rights such as to assemble peaceably and without arms; to travel throughout the country or even the right to practice any profession may be suspended.

B. FINANCIAL STABILITY

If the President of India is satisfied that a situation has arisen, whereby the financial stability or the credit of India or any part is threatened.

The effect: The Union of India may give directions to any State in respect of financial propriety. Such a direction may include reduction of salaries of government servants etc.

C. GOVERNMENT OF THE STATE CANNOT CONTINUE

If the President of India (on a report from the Governor of a State or otherwise) is satisfied that the government of the State cannot continue in accordance with the provisions of the Constitution, he may assume all the powers exercisable by the Governor of the State.

In such a case, the President himself may carry out the functions for governing the state.

8
Elections

ELECTION COMMISSION

Role

The Commission supervises and controls the preparation of electoral rolls for the elections to the Parliament, State Legislature and of the President and Vice-President of India.

Composition

The Election Commission will consist of the *Chief Election Commissioner* and certain number of Election Commissioners as the President may decide.

Advisory Role

Where a situation arises as to whether a member of either House of Parliament should be disqualified, the decision of the President is final. It is here that the Election Commission steps in. The President has to *consult* the Election Commission before arriving at any decision.

In a case where a member of the House of Legislature of a state requires to be disqualified, the decision of the Governor of the State is final. Likewise, the Governor cannot come to a decision without consulting the Election Commission.

REGIONAL COMMISSIONERS

Appointment

The President may appoint Regional Commissioners before each general election to the House of People and to the Legislative Assembly of each State.

Role

The Regional Commissioners assist the Election Commission in the performance of its functions.

Qualifications for Voting

To be entitled to vote, a person must be:

(a) a citizen of India; *and*

(b) not less than 18 years of age.

However, a person must not be otherwise disqualified on the grounds of either unsoundness of mind, non-residence etc.

9

The President, Vice-President, Council Of Ministers & Prime Minister

THE PRESIDENT OF INDIA

Election

The President is elected by the members of the electoral college consisting of:
- the elected members of Both the Houses of Parliament *and*
- elected members of the Legislative Assemblies of the states.

There must be uniformity in the scale of representation of the different states.

Qualifications

(a) Must be a citizen of India.

(b) Must have completed 35 years of age *and*

(c) Must qualify for the election as a member of the Lok Sabha.

Term of Office

The President will hold office for a term of five years from the date on which he/she enters office.

Powers of the President

All the executive powers of the Union of India are taken in his/her name. President is the 'head' of the defence forces of the country. Only the President has the power to proclaim 'emergency' in the country.

Impeachment

A President can be impeached only for violation of the Constitution.

When a President is to be impeached:

(1) a charge will be made by either House of Parliament.
(2) once a charge has been made by either House of Parliament, the other House will investigate the charge. The President has a right to appear at the charge.
(3) if, after the investigation a resolution is passed and a majority of not less than $2/3^{rd}$ of the House investigating the charge, declares that the charge against the President has been sustained, the resolution has the effect to remove the President.

THE VICE-PRESIDENT OF INDIA

Election

He is elected by the members of both Houses of Parliament at a joint meeting.

Qualifications

(a) Must be a citizen of India.
(b) Must have completed 35 years of age *and*
(c) Must qualify for the election as a member of the Council of States.

Term of Office

The Vice-President will hold office for a term of five years.

The Vice-President acts as the President when there is a vacancy in the office of the President either by death, resignation, removal or when the President is absent or suffering from illness.

COUNCIL OF MINISTERS

They form the advisory council of the President. The Prime Minister is the head of the Council of Ministers.

PRIME MINISTER

The Prime Minister is appointed by the President.

Duties

(i) To communicate to the President all decisions of the Council of Ministers.

(ii) To furnish to the President information regarding the dealings of the Union of India.

(iii) To submit any matter to the Council of Ministers, if the President feels that the decision has been taken by a Minister but not considered by the Council.

10

Judiciary

SUPREME COURT AND HIGH COURT

At the Union level we have the Supreme Court, consists of the Chief Justice of India and not more than seven judges, until Parliament by law prescribes a larger number.

Appointment of Judges of the Supreme Court

The judges are appointed by the President of India after consultation with the other judges of the Supreme Court and of the High Court and the Chief Justice of India.

Office

A Supreme Court judge can hold office until he attains the age of sixty five years.

Qualifications of a Judge of the Supreme Court

A person will not be qualified for appointment as a judge of the Supreme Court unless he is a citizen of India and :

1. has been for at least five years a judge of a High Court or of two or more such courts in succession; or
2. has been for at least ten years an advocate of a High Court or of two or

more such courts in succession; or

3. is, in the opinion of the President, a distinguished jurist.

Removal of a Judge of the Supreme Court

1. A Judge of the Supreme Court will not be removed from his office except by an order of the President, passed only after an address by each House of Parliament. It should be supported by:

    a. a majority of the total membership of that House;

    b. by a majority of not less than two-thirds of the members of that House present and voting and has been presented to the President in the same session;

    on the ground of proved misbehaviour or incapacity.

2. A Judge of the Supreme Court may also resign by submitting in writing his decision to the President.

Seat of the Supreme Court

The seat of the Supreme Court must be at Delhi or in such other place/s as the Chief Justice of India may, with the approval of the President, from time to time, appoint.

HIGH COURT

At the State level we have the High Courts for each State. Every High Court, will consist of a Chief Justice and such other Judges as the President may from time to time deem it necessary to appoint.

Appointment of Judges of the High Court

1. Every judge will be appointed by the President after consultation, with the Chief Justice of India, the Governor of the State.

2. In case of appointment of a judge other than the Chief Justice of the High Court, the President will also consult the Chief Justice of the concerned High Court.

Office

A judge shall hold office until he attains the age of sixty-two years.

Qualifications of a Judge of the High Court

A person will not be qualified for appointment as a Judge of the High Court unless he is a citizen of India and :

1. has for at least ten years held a judicial office in the territory of India; or
2. has for at least ten years been an advocate of a High Court or of two or more such courts in succession.

Vacating the Office of a Judge of the High Court

1. A Judge of the High Court may be removed in the same manner as a Judge of the supreme Court, which is discussed above.
2. The office of a judge of the High Court will also be vacated by his being appointed by the President to be a Judge of the Supreme Court or by his being transferred to any other High Court within India.
3. A Judge of the High Court may also resign from his office by submitting in writing his decision to the President.

SUBORDINATE COURTS

Appointment of a District Judge

A District Judge shall be appointed by the Governor of the concerned State in consulation with the High Court of the State.

Qualifications of a District Judge

A person can be eligible to be appointed as a district judge only if:

1. he has been for not less than seven years, an advocate or a pleader; and
2. is recommended by the High Court for appointment.

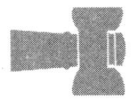 # Part VII

Other Important Provisions

Marriage & Divorce

India is a democratic country having different cultures, traditions and religious beliefs. Every Indian, whether Hindu, Muslim, Sikh, etc, is governed by his own personal laws of marriage and divorce, depending on his faith. As a result, diverse matrimonial laws prevailing in India.

CONCEPT OF MARRIAGE AND DIVORCE

MUSLIM LAW

A Muslim marriage or *nikah* is a contract made between a male & female. It is a civil contract and no priest is required for its performance.

Every Muslim who has attained puberty and who is of sound mind may enter into a contract of marriage.

Essentials of a Valid Marriage

- There should be a *proposal* made by one of the parties to the marriage and an *acceptance* of the same by, the other. Two male or one male and two female adult witnesses must be present.
- The proposal and acceptance both must be expressed at one meeting.

Dissolution

A Muslim marriage can be dissolved by the parties without taking recourse to the court, in the following ways :

(1) Talak: when the husband wants a divorce it is known as divorce by talak. It may either be revocable or irrevocable. (It can be cancelled or it becomes absolute after a certain period). There are different forms of talak: (i) talak ahsan (ii) talak hasan (iii) talak-ul-biddat. A Muslim husband may divorce his wife without assigning any cause. The wife however, must be informed of the same.

(2) Mutual Consent: divorce may take place by the mutual consent of the husband and wife. This is known as Khula or Mubaraat.

(3) Talak-i-tafweez: a Muslim wife can divorce herself from her husband if the agreement made before or after the marriage empowers her to ask for the divorce.

Women married under the Muslim law can obtain a decree for dissolution of her marriage on certain grounds. These include:

(i) where the husband has neglected or has failed to provide for the wife's maintenance for a period of two years *or*

(ii) the husband has failed to perform his marital obligations for a period of three years *or*

(iii) the husband has been insane for a period of two years etc.

HINDU LAW

According to the Vedas, a marriage is a union of flesh with flesh and bone with bone. It is a union which the Vedas regard as eternal.

Essentials of a Valid Marriage

- Age: the bridegroom and the bride should have completed the age of 21 and 18, respectively.
- Mental state: neither party to the marriage should be an idiot or lunatic at time of the marriage and must be capable of giving valid consent.
- Monogamy: neither party to the marriage should have a spouse living at the time of the marriage.

- Prohibited degree of relationship: parties should not be within such degree of a relationship where such marriages are not allowed. For instance, where parties to marriages are brother and sister, uncle and niece, aunt and nephew etc. However, if a custom or usage governing each of them permits such marriage, they may marry each other.

Dissolution

Divorce is permitted on certain serious and specific grounds to the husband and the wife, including:

(1) voluntary having sexual intercourse with another person other than his or her spouse.
(2) conversion to another religion.
(3) insanity.
(4) whereabouts not known for seven years of either party
(5) when parties to the marriage are not living together for one year after decree of restitution of conjugal rights has been passed.

PARSI LAW

Essentials of a valid Marriage

- Parties to the marriage should not be within the prohibited degree of relations. Marriages between the persons of close relations like sister and brother, aunt and nephew, uncle and niece etc. are prohibited.
- Marriage should be solemnized according to the Parsi form of ceremony prescribed for the marriage, known as *Ashirwad.*
- Presence of two Parsi witnesses, other than the priest solemnizing the marriage.
- Parsi males should have completed the age of 21 and Parsi females, the age of 18.

Dissolution

Different grounds have been recognized and made available under *The Parsi*

Marriage and Divorce Act, 1936. These include:

(1) refusal of either party to consummate the marriage within one year after solemnization.
(2) unsoundness of mind of either party.
(3) party to the marriage was pregnant by some person other than husband
(4) party to the marriage has committed adultery, bigamy rape or any unnatural offence
(5) party to the marriage is undergoing a sentence of imprisonment for seven years or more.

CHRISTIAN LAW

Essentials of a Valid Christian Marriage (Under The Indian Christian Marriage Act, 1872)

- At least one party to the marriage must be Christian.
- Marriage can be solemnized by one of the following including :
    (a) the minister of religion licensed under the act to solemnize marriages
    (b) by or in the presence of, a Marriage Registrar appointed under the Act
    (c) any person licensed under this Act to grant certificates of marriage between Indian Christians.
- Either party to the marriage must give notice according to the prescribed form. Notice should contain the details such as name, profession, the church or dwelling unit in which the marriage is to solemnized etc.

Dissolution

The Indian Divorce Act of 1869, provides certain grounds for divorce which are available to both the parties to the marriage.

A husband may present a petition to the District Court or to the High Court, requesting his marriage be dissolved on the ground that his wife, since the solemnization of the marriage has been guilty of adultery.

A wife may present a petition to the District Court or to the High Court, requesting her marriage be dissolved on certain grounds including:

(1) if her husband has converted from Christianity to some other religion and married another woman.

(2) if her husband has been guilty of rape, sodomy or bestiality, *or*

(3) of bigamy with adultery.

(4) of marriage with another women.

SPECIAL MARRIAGE ACT, 1954

The Special Marriage Act 1954, replaced the earlier legislation to provide a special form of marriage which is available to any person in India, who are in Jammu and Kashmir irrespective of the religious faith which either party to the marriage may profess.

2
Will & Probate

I. WILL

A Will, also called a testament, is a legal declaration made in a prescribed manner, stating the intention of the person making it, i.e. the *testator* or *testatrix*, with regard to their property (moveable/immoveable), which they wish to take effect after their death.

ESSENTIAL CHARACTERISTICS

Following are the essential characteristics of a Will:

- there must be a legal declaration, i.e. it must be in conformity with all the legal provisions applicable.
- the declaration must be with respect to the testator's property. It should relate to disposal of the testator's property and not merely with management of the property on a persons death.
- the declaration operates only after the death of the person making it. A Will is revocable during the testator's lifetime.
- the Will must be signed by the maker and attested by two witnesses. Once the maker signs the Will, the two witnesses must sign as *attesting witnesses*.
- a Will usually contains the name of the executor. The executor is a person appointed by the testator to ensure that the provisions of the Will are fulfilled and the intention of the testator is carried into effect after his death.

STAMP DUTY AND REGISTRATION

A Will does not need to be compulsorily registered and no stamp duty is payable on it.

WHO CAN MAKE A Will?

Any person who is in a sound and disposing state of mind, memory and understanding, at the time of making a Will is allowed to make it.

A minor is not able to make a Will.

KINDS OF WILLS

There are mainly two kinds of Wills ie, a Privileged Will and an Unprivileged Will.

A Privileged Will is executed by a person who is employed in the Defence Services. Any Will which is not Privileged, is an Unprivileged Will.

Other kinds of Wills

- Nuncupative Will : also known as Oral Will. It has to be made before a sufficient number of witnesses.
- Inofficious Will : this is a Will that appears to have been made contrary to the testators natural love and moral duties.
- Mutual Will : this means a Will executed by two testators with both the testators conferring upon each other, reciprocal benefits.
- Joint Will : this is a Will which is made by two or more testators disposing off their separate or joint property.
- Conditional Will : this refers to a Will that is contingent on the happening of a future event i.e. if the event does not happen then the Will has no effect.
- Living Will : this is usually executed by people suffering from serious ailments. It declares the treatments that they would wish to undergo or not undergo.
- Duplicate Will : this is where a will is executed in duplicate. One copy is kept with the testator while the other is kept in the custody of another

person. On the destruction of the copy in the testators possession, the Will is said to be revoked.

II. CODICIL

A Codicil is an instrument made in addition to a Will. It is used for explaining, altering or adding any of the provisions/contents in the Will and forms part of the Will.

However, it has an independent existence by itself.

A Codicil cannot be assumed to be revoked if the Will of which it is a part is revoked. A Codicil is required to be revoked separately.

III. PROBATE

Probate means a certified copy of a Will that grants to the executors of the Will the right to administer the matters provided for, in the Will.

The Will must be certified by a court having competent jurisdiction to do so.

A probate may be granted of a will as well as of a Codicil.

SPECIMEN OF A WILL

I, Mrs. Reena Kapoor, wife of Harsh Kapoor, residing at Flat No.23, American Apartments, Paris Road, Bombay, do hereby revoke all Wills/Codicils and other Testamentary dispositions which I may have heretofore made and declare this to be my last Will and Testament.

1. My husband Harsh and I have no children.
2. I hereby appoint my husband as the sole Executor of this Will and in the event of his predeceasing me I appoint my brother Mihir Khanna as the sole Executor.
3. Harsh and I are joint owners of the aforesaid Flat. I am the first holder. Both of us are also joint members of American Co-operative Housing Society Ltd. jointly holding 5 shares Nos. ____ to ____ under Certifi-

cate No. _____. Harsh and I are in exclusive joint use and possession of the said Flat. No third party has any interest in the Flat and/or shares.

4. On my death my share in the said Flat and Shares will belong absolutely to Harsh. In the event of his predeceasing me then I hereby give devise and bequeath the said Flat and Shares together with the membership rights in the said Society and the right of possession to my brother, Mihir. It is my express desire that my entire Estate do belong absolutely to Mihir.

5. I have invested some amounts in Mutual Funds and RBI Bonds, which are in my single name. All benefits, accruals in respect of the same shall belong to Harsh absolutely.

6. I hereby give devise and bequeath the rest and residue of all my properties, estates and effects including movable and immovable, if any, wherever situate to Harsh absolutely and in the event of his predeceasing me I bequeath the same to Mihir in the manner aforesaid.

7. I am making this will of my own free will and accord and in a sound and disposing state of mind, memory and understanding.

Bombay, this _____ day of _____, 2004

SIGNED SEALED AND PUBLISHED	)
by the withinnamed Testatrix Reena	)
Kapoor as her Last Will and Testament	)
in the presence of us both who were present	)
at the same time and at her request and	)
in the presence of each other have set and	)
subscribed our respective signatures as	)
attesting witnesses	)

1.
2.

3

Duties Of A Lawyer

Just as a doctor has certain duties towards a person under his care and treatment, a lawyer too, has certain duties towards the court as well as his/her clients.

A lawyer must, at all times, conduct himself in a manner befitting his status as an officer of the court. He is a privileged member of the community.

A. DUTIES TOWARDS THE COURT

(i) Respect: a lawyer must maintain a respectful attitude towards the court, bearing in mind that the dignity of the judicial office is essential for our community and society.

(ii) Relatives: an advocate cannot appear in a court or before an authority, if the judge or officer is related to the advocate as father, grandfather, son, grandson, uncle, brother, nephew, first cousin, husband, wife, mother, daughter, sister, aunt, niece or in-laws.

(iii) Dress code: an advocate must not wear bands or his gown in public places. He can only wear them in places where the court or the Bar Council of India may allow. Also, he must appear in court only in the prescribed dress.

(iv) Illegal or improper means: an advocate cannot influence the decision of a Court by any illegal or improper means. He is prohibited from privately communicating with the Judge in relation to a pending case.

(v) Financial interest: an advocate should not involve himself in any matter in which he has a financial interest.

(vi) Director : an Advocate must not accept a case from a Company of which he is a director.

B. DUTIES TOWARDS THE CLIENT

(i) Withdrawal from a case : an advocate cannot withdraw from a case once he has accepted it, unless there is a sufficient reason for doing so and he has informed his client well in advance.

(ii) Upholding the client's interest : it is the advocate's duty to fearlessly uphold the interest of his client by all fair and honourable means. He must defend a person accused of a crime regardless of his own personal opinion regarding the accused.

(iii) Instructions : an advocate must not act on instructions of any person other than his client or his client's duly authorized agent.

(iv) Lending money : an advocate must not lend money to his client for the purpose of any legal proceeding for which he has been engaged by his client.

(v) Fees: an advocate can neither stipulate a fee depending upon the outcome of the matter, nor can he share the spoils of the litigation in which he was engaged.

(vi) Witness: an advocate must not accept a matter in which he believes he may be a witness.

- An advocate is a professional. He is not allowed to solicit work or advertise, either directly or indirectly by circulars, advertisements, interviews etc. whereby he 'markets' himself.

C. DUTIES TOWARDS OPPONENTS

An advocate must not communicate or negotiate with the other party to the matter, when the other party is represented by an advocate. So also, he shall do his best to carry out all legitimate promises made to the opposite party.

4

Law Of Limitation

MEANING

Limitation refers to the time limit within which an action may be brought about, or some act be done, to safeguard a certain right.

An aggrieved person has a *right* to enforce the law against someone he has a grievance against. He must exercise his *remedy* within the time limit allowed by the law. If he fails to do so, then he loses that remedy forever. There are certain exceptions to this rule as well.

■ Example : Amar wants to evict a person who has been staying in his property for sometime. Amar has legal recourses available to him, to remove this person, for instance, by filing a suit. However, Amar delays the filing of the suit beyond the time provided by the law. In such a case the remedy available to Amar of filing a suit is lost. However, his right continues to exist and he could take recourse under another provision of the law, to enforce his rights.

FILING AN APPLICATION/APPEAL

Generally, an appeal or any application *may* be allowed by the court, after the specified time limit, if the person making the appeal/application offers to the court, sufficient reason as to why he was unable to make the same within the time limit.

MINORITY

What happens when a person entitled to file a suit/application, is a minor at the time when the period of limitation is to begin?

In such a case, the law allows the minor to file his suit or application after his disability has ceased to exist. In other words, the time limit begins to run as soon as he becomes a major.

■ Example : Raj (16 years) has become entitled to institute a suit by reason of being a legal representative of his uncle. He can file the suit on becoming 18 years old. The time limit is to be taken into consideration once Raj attains the age of 18 years. It is immaterial whether Raj has a guardian at that time or not.

ACKNOWLEDGEMENT OF A DEBT IN WRITING

What is the effect of an acknowledgement (admission) of a liability by a party?

We are aware that the law prescribes a certain period for filing of suits, complaints etc. The principle of an acknowledgement in writing means that if, before the expiry of the period of limitation, an acknowledgment in writing is made and signed by the party against whom the claim is made, the period of limitation is then to be reckoned from the time when the acknowledgement was made.

■ Example: Abhay had a money claim of Rs. 5,00,000/- against Rupam. The latest by which he could institute his suit was July, 2003. Thereafter, he will lose his remedy by way of a suit. However, on April 23, 2003, Rupam sent a cheque for Rs. 50,000/- in favour of Abhay along with a letter (of even date) stating that this cheque was in part payment of the amount of Rs. 5,00,000/- he owed Abhay. The period of limitation is now to be computed from date of the cheque/letter.

ADVERSE POSSESSION

When a person is in possession of a property adverse to that of a lawful owner for a period of more than twelve years, he is entitled to certain rights in respect of that property. He gets a title equal to that of the property's owner. Further, the law also takes away the remedy of the lawful owner to claim in respect of the property, while giving a good title to the person who is in its possession. Such a person may be a trespasser as well.

CRITERIA

The person (owner by adverse possession) must satisfy certain requirements to enable him to get the benefit of this provision of law. These include :

- continuous possession, wherein, the trespasser or the person who claims adverse possession must be in continuous or uninterrupted possession.
- the lawful owner must be aware of such possession.
- mere entry of a name in the property card is not sufficient to prove adverse possession.
- this provision does not apply to a person who has a lawful title to the property.
- onus : the owner by adverse possession has to prove that the plaintiff (or rightful owner) was dispossessed for more than 12 years.

5

Arbitration

INTRODUCTION

In ancient India, decisions of the *panchayats* (consisting of wealthy, influential and elderly men of the community) were recognized and were to be obeyed. The *panchayats* were entrusted with the power of management and the sanctions against disobedience to their decisions were severe.

The East India Company framed regulations regarding arbitration

ARBITRATION

Arbitration is a reference regarding the decision of one or more persons in respect to a particular matter between the parties.

It is a substitution by consent (agreement) of the parties of another court, other than the ones provided under the ordinary process of law. The persons who give their decision (judgment) on the reference are the *arbitrators*. However, parties cannot by contract oust jurisdiction of courts.

ARBITRATION AGREEMENT

It is an agreement between the parties to submit for arbitration, <u>disputes</u> which have arisen or which may arise between them.

REQUIREMENTS

1. It may form a part of an agreement in the form of an arbitration clause or there may be a separate arbitration agreement.
2. It has to be in writing, either in the form of a document signed by the parties.

Note : An arbitration agreement stands void if a party to the agreement is a minor or is a person of unsound mind. This is a ground for setting aside an award. Further, if the object of the contract is unlawful, the arbitration agreement will be void.

■ Example : Akhil entered into an agreement with Brijendra to purchase arms and ammunition to sell them to a national enemy. A contract of this nature is illegal. The arbitration agreement which forms a part of this agreement is void and unenforceable.

AWARD

An award is the final determination of a claim or a part of it by the Arbitral Tribunal. The Arbitral Tribunal may consist of a single arbitrator or a panel of arbitrators.

INTERNATIONAL COMMERCIAL ARBRITATION

This applies when one of the parties is a foreigner either a foreign national or resident or a foreign company whose central management is in foreign hands.

■ Example: ABC Company Private Limited (India) entered into an agreement to render consultancy services to an international company, Boeing Aviation Limited for the sale of aircrafts in India. The foreign company did not pay the Indian company for its services. The parties can refer their dispute under international commercial arbitration.

EXTENT OF JUDICIAL INTERVENTION

The courts are restrained from interfering in disputes when there is an arbitration agreement between the parties.

However, the court has the power to:

- pass interim orders as measures of protection.
- set aside an award passed by the arbitrator.
- A criminal complaint cannot be referred for arbitration.
- Matrimonial matters too, cannot be referred for arbitration.

COMPOSITION OF ARBITRAL TRIBUNAL

The number of arbitrators will be decided by the parties. The number must not be even.

APPOINTMENT OF ARBITRATORS

1. A person of any nationality may become an arbitrator.
2. The parties can decide the procedure for appointment of arbitrator.
3. In an arbitration involving three arbitrators, each party will appoint one arbitrator and the two appointed arbitrators will appoint the third arbitrator, who will act as the *presiding arbitrator.*
4. However, if the party fails to appoint an arbitrator within a period of 30 days from the receipt of a request by the other party *or* if the two appointed arbitrators fail to appoint a presiding arbitrator within 30 days of their appointment, the Chief Justice shall make the appointment.
5. When appointing an arbitrator, the court has no power to go into the pros and cons of the case.

GROUNDS TO CHALLENGE THE AUTHORITY OF THE ARBITRATOR

An arbitrator's authority may be challenged only if there are doubts concerning his independence or impartiality *or* if he does not possess the necessary qualifications agreed to by the parties.

A party to the arbitration can challenge his own appointee but only on the ground of which he became aware *after* the appointment.

■ Example : In an arbitration between two parties (A and B), each appoint an arbitrator (C and D respectively), and the two arbitrators appoint a presiding arbitrator. A later discovers that arbitrator C was related to party B. Party A is entitled to challenge the appointment of arbitrator C on this ground since he became aware after the appointment that arbitrator C is related to party B.

PLACE OF ARBRITRATION

The place of arbitration will be determined by the arbitrators if the parties are unable to agree on a place.

COMMENCEMENT OF AN ARBRITATION PROCEEDING

An arbritation proceeding is said to commence on the date on which a request for the dispute to be referred for arbitration is received by the other party (i.e. the person against whom the relief has been claimed).

PROCEDURE

Within the time provided by the tribunal, the claimant will file his 'statement of claim' and the respondent (the person against whom the relief is claimed), his 'written statement'.

The arbitrator may terminate the proceedings where the claimant fails to file his statement of claim in time without 'sufficient reasons'.

When the respondent fails to submit his defence, the proceedings continue without treating the failure as an admission.

CONTENTS OF AN ARBITRAL AWARD

1. It is to be in writing and signed by the members of the arbitral tribunal. The award must state the reasons on which it is given, unless the parties agree that no reasons are to be given.
2. A signed copy of the award is to be delivered to each party.
3. The award must state the date and place of arbitration.
4. The tribunal may, at any time during the proceedings, make an interim award.

Successive Awards: there may be as many awards as there are disputes out of the contract.

An award becomes binding after three months from the date of receipt of award by the parties, unless an application has been made to the court for setting aside the award.

CORRECTION AND INTERPRETATION OF AN AWARD

Within 30 days from the receipt of an award, a party may request the tribunal to *correct* any errors in the award or may request the tribunal to give an *interpretation* of a specific point or part of the award.

The errors referred to are *clerical errors* and not errors of judgment.

AN ARBITRAL AWARD CAN BE SET ASIDE BY THE COURT, IF :

the party filing the application furnishes proof that:

(a) the party was under some incapacity *or*

(b) the agreement of arbitration is not valid *or*

(c) improper notice regarding the appointment of arbitrator is furnished *or*

(d) the award deals with a dispute not contemplated under the reference.

or

If the court finds:

(a) the subject matter is not capable of being settled by arbitration (for instance, under the rent law) *or*

(b) the award is in conflict with the public policy of India.

Application is to be made within three months of the award.

ENFORCEMENT OF AN AWARD

An award can be enforced as if it were a decree of the court.

REGISTRATION OF AN AWARD

Where an award is for the payment of a sum of money by one party to another, it does not require registration. When an award appears to create, extinguish, assign, declare any right, title or interest in immoveable property of Rs. 100/- or upwards, it requires registration.

An award is chargeable to stamp duty.

SPECIMEN OF AN ARBRITATION CLAUSE

Any dispute or difference arising out of or in connection with this agreement shall be submitted to arbitration to a sole arbitrator, appointed by agreement between the parties, under the Arbitration and Conciliation Act, 1996. In the event the Parties are unable to agree on a sole arbitrator within 30 days of a notice served on one party by the other, then each party shall appoint one arbitrator and the arbitrators so appointed shall appoint the third arbitrator. The place of arbitration shall be Chennai and the language of arbitration shall be in English.

6

Right To Information

INTRODUCTION

India is a democratic nation. Every individual has a right to know. Every citizen has a right to information. It is this right of information that informs and assists us in understanding how our government, public institutions and public sector undertakings function.

MEANING

It is the right to access information which is held by, or under the control of any public authority. It includes the right to:

(i) inspection of work, documents and records.

(ii) take notes, extracts or certified copies of documents or records.

(iii) take certified samples of material.

(iv) obtain information in the form of diskettes, floppies, tapes, video cassettes or other electronic modes or through printouts where such information is stored in a computer or in any other device.

THE AUTHORITIES FROM WHOM INFORMATION CAN BE DEMANDED

Information can be demanded from all public authorities including all government bodies and organizations substantially financed by the government including NGOs.

The Right to Information Act, 2005 and the rules framed under the Act prescribe the following:

- an application to be made by the applicant (i.e. the person who needs the information) as per a specific format to call for information.
- the time limit within which the information desired must be provided i.e. within 30 days.
- the manner in which information is provided. Citizens can ask for information and get copies of the required documents.
- makes a distinction between information which can be given and the information which will not be provided.
- the fee that will be charged when seeking the information.
- citizens also have a right to inspect documents/files at the concerned offices between the prescribed office timings.
- the administrative offices of public authorities to appoint Public Information Officer or PIO.
- remedy : if the information desired is not provided or wrongly refused then – the citizen can prefer an appeal.
- delay: a penalty of Rs. 250 is levied on the PIO for everyday delay in providing the necessary information.

INFORMATION WHICH CAN BE DENIED

There is no obligation on the part of the state to give information, which:

- would affect the sovereignty, integrity, security and safety of the state or country.
- will compromise the strategic, economic and scientific interests of the state or nation.
- any court/tribunal has expressly forbidden from being given.
- includes commercial confidence, trade secrets, the disclosure of which would

harm a third party.
- is received from a foreign government.
- would endanger the life or physical safety of any person.
- will impede the prosecution of offenders.

AN INSTANCE OF HOW THE RIGHT TO INFORMATION WAS USED

A gentleman by the name of Bhimsen Sharma applied for a gas connection. Every time he inquired about the status of his connection, he was asked to come back later. He had also observed that there were others who applied for the connection much after him but obtained it sooner. Bhimsen Sharma made an application under the Act to the concerned PIO of the relevant department. In his application he requisitioned for information viz.: up to what date the applications for gas connections have been cleared, the reasons for the delay and a copy of the register showing date wise, the applications made and connections alloted. This will reveal if the authorities had sanctioned connections to persons who applied later, and for which they would have no justification. Mr. Sharma promptly returned home with the gas connection.

7
Human Rights

DEFINITION

Human rights include all those rights which are fundamental for the existence of mankind anywhere in the state, the country or the world. Every human being has a right to live with dignity and respect. Correspondingly, he has to respect and take care of the needs of others as well.

HISTORY

The history of human rights date back to the year 1215, when the subjects of King John, the King of England asked him to sign the 'Magna Carta' or the Great Charter and the Bill of Rights, in around 1689.

Movements like Swaraj were started by our great national leader, viz. Bal Gangadhar Tilak.

MEANING

Human rights extend from moral rights to cultural, educational, legal and even religious rights. They also include the right to life, right to practice trade, right to practice religion etc. These are the rights guaranteed by the Constitution of India.

Man plays various roles in society, such as an employer, employee, consumer, worker, religious believer, tourist, etc. In all these respects, human rights apply.

■ Example : As a consumer a person has the right to purchase a product of good quality in exchange for money. He is also entitled to good quality services for a price. As a religious person or a devotee, he is entitled to enter a place of worship.

As a labourer in a factory, he has a right to safe working environment.

HUMAN RIGHTS ACT

The Human Rights Act, 1993 was enacted to promote and protect human rights at the state level as well as the national level.

At the state level, the State Human Rights Commission has been set up. The National Human Rights Commission has been established at the national level.

ROLE OF THE COMMISSION

(i) To inquire into any complaint made by a victim or any person on his behalf regarding violation of human rights or the negligence in preventing such rights by a public servant. The commission can take action on its own initiative as well.

(ii) To visit any jail or any other institution where persons are detained or lodged for treatment, protection, reformation etc. with intimation to the government.

(iii) To intervene in any court proceeding (with the approval of such court) where any proceeding is pending, involving any violation of human rights.

(iv) To study treaties and other international instruments and conventions on human rights and make representations on the same.

(v) To promote research in the field of human rights.

(vi) To spread human rights literacy among various sections of the society.

(vii) To encourage the efforts of Non-governmental Organisations (NGO) in the field of human rights.

(viii) To educate society regarding the importance of human rights since ignorance is a constant threat to human rights. Through education and awareness, human rights can be far more effective.

ILL-TREATMENT OF PRISONERS

Newspapers and television channels champion causes against torture of prisoners, custodial death, ill-treatment of prisoners etc. The Human Rights Commission has notably played a crucial role in protecting the victims of such violation.

8

Intellectual Property Rights

TRADEMARK

A trademark means :

(a) a mark capable of being represented graphically *and*
(b) which is capable of distinguishing the goods and services of one person from those of others.

At times, the shape of goods may constitute a trademark. Services too, have been included under the scope of trademarks.

Services may include: banking, financing, communication, real estate, insurance, entertainment, news etc.

A trade mark must bear a unique character.

It is advisable to have the trademark registered. Registration gives an exclusive right to its owner to use the trademark in respect of the goods and services for which it is registered.

Any person who commits any offence is liable to be punished.

COPYRIGHTS

To explain the term we will start with an example:

■ A Bollywood film had released a music album of its songs. ABC Music

Limited wanted to acquire the rights to the film music. It approached the makers of the film and purchased the rights to the music for a large sum of money.

The film owner's music rights or copyrights have actually been purchased by the music company.

Copyright protects the rights of the legal owner of the copyright and provides him with recourse in law against unauthorized user.

Let us take another example:

■ Sharadbhai is a script writer for cinematographic films. He has a copyright on his scripts. Each time Sharadbhai prepares a script, he registers it with the Film Writers Association and gets a proof of registration for the same. On one such occasion, he registered a script relating to how a family gets divided during a war with the neighbouring country. Few months later, he found that a movie was being made on the lines of his script with a similar climax. Sharadbhai is entitled by law to an action against the makers of the new film since he has a copyright over the script.

- Artistic works, music, films etc. can all be copyrighted.

PATENTS

Only an invention can be patented. What is not an invention does not qualify for a patent.

The following does not amount to an invention:
- an invention which is false.
- method of agriculture.
- presentation of information.

9

Public Interest Litigation (PIL)

A Public Interest Litigation is an action taken in a court of law for resolving issues relating to the general public or society at large. The powers to initiate action by way of a PIL are provided under the Constitution of our country.

INSTANCES

A PIL may be filed (1) when the safety/security of the people of India is under threat - for instance when acts of terrorism have threatened the peace of the State; (2) where human rights are violated, such as if the inmates in jails and prisons are ill-treated; (3) where religious sentiments or rights are violated etc.

WHO CAN FILE A PIL?

Any person who is interested or concerned for the welfare of persons, society etc. but who cannot approach the court may prefer a PIL. It is not necessary that the person who has filed the PIL must be directly affected by the wrong or injustice that is complained of.

A PIL is not a medium of redressing personal disputes.

■ Example : If an individual has a monetary claim against another, he cannot maintain an action by way of a PIL.

AGAINST WHOM CAN A PIL BE FILED?

A PIL may be filed against any authority who has a statutory duty to perform an act.

A PIL may be filed to move the authority to perform its duty when it has failed and/or neglected to perform its duty *or*

To prevent the concerned authority from excessive use of its powers or authority.

For instance, A PIL may be filed against the municipal corporation if it has failed to take care of drainage in a particular locality; Action by way of a PIL may be initiated against a government or the authorities under it, where the authority has failed to do its duty required under law.

Generally, a PIL is not filed against a private party. However, when action is contemplated by way of a PIL, against a private party, the private party along with the statutory authority can be made parties to the petition.

■ Example : The laboratory of a hospital had been disposing excessive garbage (which contains used syringes, broken bottles, waste food, medicines, acids etc.) in an area which was causing harm to people nearby and affecting their living conditions. A PIL was filed against the local municipal corporation and the hospital as well.

A PIL is filed in Court in the same manner, as a writ petition.

10

Protection Of Wild Life

INTRODUCTION

A rapid decline in the number and species of wild animals and birds led to the introduction of *The Wild Life Protection Act, 1972*. Ecological imbalances, poaching etc. have been the main causes of this decline. Certain species of wild animals and birds are already extinct in our country. Animals such as cheetahs are not found in India anymore.

Tigers too are on their way to extinction due to poaching. Tigers are hunted for their skin and nails and to be preserved as trophies. In earlier times, the kings and members of royal families would go on a tiger hunt with a full entourage consisting of soldiers, elephants, horses etc. Killing a tiger was considered a sign of manliness.

Being our national animal, it will be strange if the tiger does indeed becomes extinct. The jungle will be minus its King.

The situation is so serious that the Prime Minister intervened and formed special investigation agencies to preserve tigers in the wild life parks and ordered a crackdown on poaching. Tigers and other predators are extremely useful when it comes to maintaining the ecological balance.

Let us understand the meaning of certain words and phrases that we associate with wild life.

(i) HUNTING

This includes:

(a) capturing, killing or poisoning any wild animal and every attempt to do the same.

(b) injuring or destroying or taking any body part of any such animal. In the case of birds or reptiles, it includes damaging the nests or eggs of the birds or reptiles.

- The law prohibits the hunting of wild animals. However, hunting is permitted when any wild animal is dangerous *to human survival or is disabled beyond recovery*. In such a case, the animal can be hunted after obtaining the necessary permission.

- It must be noted that hunting itself is an offence and any attempt to hunt is also punishable. However, killing of an animal in self defense is not an offence.

■ Example: The Nair family was on their way to a nearby hill station from Bangalore. Their car broke down on the way, in a deserted area. Out of nowhere two wild boars appeared and were preparing to attack the Nairs. The Nairs who were carrying some glass bottles broke a few of them, attacked the wild animals and killed them. No offence has been committed since the act of hunting was in self defense.

(ii) PROTECTED AREA

This refers to national parks, sanctuaries, conservation reserves etc.

(iii) TROPHY

This means the whole or part of any captive or wild animal, other than vermin, which has been kept or preserved by any means, whether artificially or naturally and includes:

(a) rugs, skins and specimens of such animal.

(b) antlers, bones, horns, tusks, eggs, nests etc.

(iv) WILD LIFE

This includes any animal, bees, butterflies, moths, fish, aquatic or land vegetation which forms a part of any habitat.

(v) WEAPONS

This includes ammunition, bows, arrows, firearms, nets, poison and any thing capable of anaesthetizing, decoying, destroying, injuring or killing an animal.

11

Equal Opportunities For Persons With Disabilities

According to the census carried out by the Government of India in 2001, there are over two crore disabled people in the country.

It therefore, becomes important to know the kinds of disabilities, the rights of disabled persons, concessions by the State/Central Government given to disabled persons etc.

MEANING

Disability includes:

(i) blindness.

(ii) low vision

(iii) leprosy-cured.

(iv) hearing impairment.

(v) locomotor disability. This means disability of the bones, joints or muscles leading to substantial restriction of the movement of the limbs or any form of cerebral palsy.

(vi) mental retardation.

(vii) mental illness.

Persons with disability means a person suffering from not less than 40% of any disability as certified by a medical authority.

CENTRAL CO-ORDINATION COMMITTEE (CCC)

Constituted by the Central Government, the CCC consists of ministers, members of Parliament and a host of highly qualified and well respected members, including directors of the National Institute of Visually Handicapped, Mentally Handicapped etc.

FUNCTIONS

(a) To serve as a national focal point on disability matters and facilitate the continuous evolution of a comprehensive policy towards solving the problems faced by persons with disabilities.
(b) To review activities of government departments and governmental and non-governmental organizations.
(c) To take up causes with international agencies.
(d) To take steps for a barrier-free environment.

STATE CO-ORDINATION COMMITTEE (SCC)

At the state level, the constitution and role of the SCC is similar to that of the CCC.

PREVENTION AND EARLY DETECTION

The appropriate governments and the local authorities, in an attempt to prevent the occurrence of disabilities, must undertake surveys, screen children at least once every year, have campaigns and create awareness in schools and other centers, take measures for natal and pre-natal care of mother and child etc.

EDUCATION

The appropriate governments and the local authorities must ensure that every child with disability has access to free education until he reaches the age of 18. Further, they must endeavor to promote integration of students with disabilities in the normal schools, as well.

EMPLOYMENT

The appropriate governments must *identify* posts in establishments which can be reserved for persons with disability.

Every appropriate government must appoint, in every establishment, not less than 3% of persons or class of persons with disabilities, of which 1% will be reserved for persons suffering from:

(a) blindness or low vision.
(b) hearing impairment.
(c) locomotor disability or cerebral palsy.

SPECIAL EMPLOYMENT EXCHANGE (SEE)

The appropriate government may require employers to give information regarding vacancies for persons with disabilities that are available or are soon to be available to the SEE. Employers must maintain records.

The SEE is an office established and maintained by the government for the collection and furnishing of information either by keeping registers or otherwise, in matters relating to:

(i) prospective employers seeking to engage employees.
(ii) persons with disabilities seeking employment.
(iii) vacancies where persons with disabilities can be appointed.

SCHEMES FOR ENSURING EMPLOYMENT OF THE DISABLED

The appropriate governments and the local authorities must, by notification, formulate schemes for ensuring employment of persons with disabilities and provide for relaxation of upper age limits, health and safety measures, training and welfare etc, of such persons.

RESERVATION IN EDUCATIONAL INSTITUTIONS

All government educational institutions and other educational institutions receiving aid from the government must reserve at least 3% seats for persons with disabilities.

Equal Opportunities For Persons With Disabilities

The appropriate governments and the local authorities must, by notification, formulate schemes in favour of persons with disabilities for *preferential allotment of land* at concessional rates for houses, setting up businesses, establishment of special schools etc.

NON-DISCRIMINATION IN ROAD AND TRANSPORT

The establishments in the transport sector must, for the benefit of persons with disabilities, adapt rail compartments, buses, aircrafts etc. in such a way, so as to permit easy access to such persons.

The appropriate governments and the local authorities must provide for the installation of auditory signals at red lights for persons with visual handicap, engraving of the surface of the zebra crossing etc.

NON-DISCRIMINATION IN GOVERNMENT EMPLOYMENT

No establishment can dispense with, or reduce in rank, an employee who acquires a disability during his service. If he is not suitable for the post, he could be shifted to another post with the same pay scale and service benefits. If it is still not possible to adjust the employee, he may be kept on a supernumerary post until a suitable post is available or until he attains the age of super annuation, whichever is earlier.

So also, no promotion can be denied to any person merely on the ground of his disability.

UNEMPLOYMENT ALLOWANCE

The appropriate governments must, by notification, formulate schemes for payment of an unemployment allowance to persons with disabilities registered with the SEE for more than two years but who could not be placed in any gainful occupation.

DISABILITY CERTIFICATES (DC)

These are issued by the Medical Board constituted by the Central and State Governments.

No DC can be refused without the applicant being given an opportunity of being heard.

Advantages: a DC will make the person eligible to apply for facilities, concessions and benefits admissible under schemes of the government and non-governmental organisations.

The Chief Commissioner for Persons with Disabilities is the authority to approach for any complaints. The complaint must be presented to him by the complainant or can be sent by registered post.

12

Settlement Of Disputes

In any case, if the court is of the opinion that a settlement is possible, it deals with that case in the following manner :

- In other words, if the judge is of the opinion that there exist certain elements of a settlement for the case which may be acceptable to the parties, the court will put together the terms of the settlement.
- These terms will be handed over to the parties for their consideration.
- After considering the terms of settlement proposed by the court, the parties to the case, will submit the terms along with their suggestions to the court.
- Once the court receives the proposed settlement along with the observations of the respective parties to the case, the court will reformulate the terms of a possible settlement.
- The Court will refer the same for any of the following :
  (a) arbitration.
  (b) conciliation.
  (c) judicial settlement
  (d) mediation.

13

Contempt Of Court

Contempt of court takes place when disrespect is caused to the court. Contempt of Court can be either *civil* or *criminal.*

- CIVIL CONTEMPT – takes place when

(1) an intentional disobedience is caused to any order, process etc. of a court *or*

(2) intentional breach of an undertaking given to a court has taken place.

- CRIMINAL CONTEMPT

This means a publication by words – spoken or written, signs or any other act which either :

(i) lowers (in any way) the authority of a court.
(ii) interferes with any court proceeding .
(iii) obstructs the administration of justice.

■ Example: A well fought battle between two parties was in progress before a senior judge of a court. A newspaper article made it very obvious that the judge who was trying the case had a reputation of indulging in unethical and corrupt practices. An action for contempt is formed in this case.

Innocent Publication - means a publication that does not amount to contempt

Contempt Of Court

of court.

If a person who is unaware of a pending court case publishes any matter which interferes with that court case, he will not be guilty of the offence of contempt of court.

Fair Criticism

A person is not guilty of publishing any fair comment on the merits of any case, which has been heard and finally decided.

■ Example : A newspaper publishes a fair assessment of its views on a recently concluded court case. The article also contains quotes from leading lawyers and retired judges in respect to the case. No case of contempt of court can be made out against the newspaper.

Punishment

An offence of contempt of court may be punishable with simple imprisonment which may extend up to six months or fine which may be up to Rs. 2,000/- or both, depending on the facts of each particular case.

Time Limit

A court cannot initiate any proceedings for contempt either itself or otherwise after a year from the date of the complaint of contempt.

14
Appeal

In legal parlance, an appeal means the removal of a case from a lower or inferior court to a superior court or forum in order to test the correctness of the decision of such lower or inferior court.

That is to say, if a party to a case in the lower court is not satisfied or is aggrieved with the decision of that court then he can file an appeal in a superior court against the 'decision' of the lower court. The superior court will then decide upon the case.

FORM OF APPEAL

Every appeal is to be preferred in the form of a memorandum signed by the appellant (person who prefers the appeal) or his advocate. It is to be submitted to the court or the proper officer as appointed by the court. The appeal must be accompanied by a copy of the judgment (the decision of the court).

- Contents of the memorandum of an appeal - the precise reasons for the objections regarding the decision of the lower court are to be stated in the memorandum.

- Where the appeal is against a decision that requires the appellant to pay money, he has to deposit the 'disputed' amount in court or furnish security as the court may direct.

■ Example : Ameya, a businessman had filed a suit against Vipul for recovery of the sum of Rs. 25,00,000/-. The court, in its decision ordered Vipul to pay the amount of Rs. 25,00,000/- to Ameya. According to Vipul, nothing was payable to Ameya. Therefore, he decided to challenge the court's order in a higher court. Vipul was asked to deposit the amount of Rs. 25,00,000/- by the court at the time of filing his appeal.

POWERS OF A COURT OF APPEAL

Generally the powers of a Court of Appeal are:

(i) the final conclusion of a case.

(ii) to remand a case back to the lower court, if it so feels necessary.

(iii) to establish the points of contention between the parties.

(iv) to take additional evidence or require such evidence to be taken.

A second appeal may be filed in certain circumstances when the aggrieved party is not satisfied with the outcome of the first appeal.

WHEN DOES AN APPEAL LIE TO THE SUPREME COURT?

An appeal lies from a decision of the High Court in a civil proceeding, if the High Court certifies that the case involves:

(a) substantial issues of law which are of importance to the public, *and*

(b) the High Court is of the opinion that the case needs to be decided by the Supreme Court.

15

Suit By Or Against The Government

In a suit by or against the government, the authority to be named as a plaintiff or defendant will be:

A. In the case of a suit by or against the Central Government, the authority to be named is the *Union of India*.

B. In the case of a suit by or against the State Government, the authority to be named is *the State*.

Plaintiff : is the person who initiates the legal action.

Defendant : is the one against whom the legal action is filed and who defends the same.

The person giving the notice and filing the suit must be one and the same.

PROCEDURE

Before a suit is instituted against the government or any public officer in respect of any act done by him in his official capacity, a notice must be given. The suit can be filed only after two months have expired after the notice in writing has been given.

- Where a suit is to be filed against the *Central Government* (except railways), the notice must be sent to a *secretary* of that Government.

- In the case of a suit against the Central Government where it relates to railways, notice must be addressed to the *general manager* of that railway.
- In the case of suit against the State Government, the notice must be issued to that *government* or the *collector* of that district.
- In a suit against a *public officer*, notice must be delivered to him or left at his office.

IMMEDIATE OR URGENT RELIEF

To obtain urgent relief against the government or a public officer, a suit may be instituted with the permission of the court. No notice (as mentioned above) is required. However, the court will not grant any relief unless the government/public officer has been given a reasonable opportunity to be heard and to present his case.

■ Example : M/s. AB Foods entered into an agreement with the State Government where AB Foods was to supply grains to the government in exchange for the price of the goods. Although the grains supplied were of proper quality and quantity, the government failed to make payment as agreed. M/s. AB Foods issued a notice for non-payment by the government. After the expiry of two months, a suit for recovery of the money was instituted by AB Foods against the government.

16

Evidence

Evidence revolves around facts. It forms an important part of a case when an accusation/allegation or defence requires to be established.

EVIDENCE INCLUDES:

(1) all statements which the court permits or requires to be made before it by witnesses in relation to matters of fact in a case. This is known as *oral evidence.*

(2) all documents that are produced for inspection of the court. This is known as *documentary evidence.*

FACTS

- A fact means the state of things or the relation of things that are capable of being perceived by the senses.
- Any mental condition of which a person is conscious.

■ Example : That you are reading this particular topic at this time, is a fact.

RELEVANT FACTS

When one fact is connected to another in a certain way, they are said to be *relevant* to one another.

■ Example : A school teacher was accused of beating up a student. On a complaint filed by the student, facts such as, what was spoken or done by the teacher and/or the student that led to the the incident and even what happened later were considered, since they were relevant facts.

When facts which are not otherwise relevant become relevant.

Facts become relevant when they make the existence or non-existence of any relevant fact highly probable or improbable.

■ Example: In continuation of the above example: Let us suppose that the accusation is that teacher (A) beat up student (B) on December 12 , 2005 at 11.00 a.m. However, from the records maintained with the office it was found that teacher A had made an application for leave (on December 1, 2005) and the leave was sanctioned, for him to visit his native place from December 10, 2005 for five days. The fact that the teacher was in his native place on the alleged day is relevant as it renders highly improbable that he was anywhere around the incident complained of.

ADMISSION

An admission is a statement (in oral or documented form) which suggests any presumption of an important fact regarding the case.

Statements made by a party to a proceeding, or by his duly authorized agent can be considered as admissions.

- No confession made to a police officer can be proved against a person accused of any offence.

EXPERTS

When the court has to form an opinion for instance under a point of any science or art or as to the identify handwriting etc., the opinions of persons who are specially skilled in such matters are relevant facts. They are called *experts*.

■ Example: The point in dispute before the court was whether the Will of Mrs. Briganza was, in fact, signed by her or whether her signature was forged. The court engaged the services of Mr. Shantilal who is a handwriting expert to determine whether the will was signed as alleged or was not so signed. The expert's report in this matter will be relevant to the case.

DOCUMENTARY PROOF

Contents of documents may be proved either by primary evidence or secondary evidence.

- Primary evidence applies:
    (1) where the document can itself be produced for inspection of the court it is primary evidence.
    (2) where a document is executed in counterpart then each counterpart of the document is primary evidence as against that person who has executed the counterpart. So also, when a number of documents are made by one uniform process, each is primary evidence of the rest.

■ Example : An actor accused a newspaper of defaming him. It is sufficient if the actor produces the implied article..

- Secondary evidence includes:
    (1) copies made from the original document.
    (2) counterparts of documents as against parties who did not execute them.

WITNESSES

A person who has observed the happening of a certain event may be a witness. The court allows all persons to give evidence before it, unless it feels that they are unable to understand the questions put to them or incapable of giving normal answers to the questions. Such inability may be on account of old age, disease etc.

- A witness who is unable to speak may give his evidence by writing or by signs. It is important that the writings or signs must be made in open court.

17

Film & Television Agreements

It has taken fifty years for the entertainment industry to obtain an 'industry status' from the government, which in turn, means that the largest film producing country in the world had, for a long time, run on self created laws and paths. No real importance was given to rules and contracts then, and every individual - whether artist, producer, director, etc. relied on trust and faith to carry forward his venture. However, today, with the entry of the corporate culture into the entertainment world, things are changing drastically and at a furious pace. The industry is realizing the value of legal documentation at every stage. Television companies are also following suit. In this chapter, after a brief discussion on the necessity for legal documentation in film contracts, certain specimen contracts have been added.

Usually, every cinematographic film has a Producer who invests his money into creating the "content". The producer will sell his content for the purpose of commercial exploitation to a Distributor. While creating the content, he will engage the services of numerous Talents. Every agreement that is signed between the parties (viz. the artists, the producer and distributors) has to be looked into with a lot of great care and attention and the terms of the contract are advisable to be duly recorded in writing, to deal with any unforeseen circumstances in the future.

In the case of television contracts too, a content is created. This content is then sold for the purposes of commercial exploitation to a television channel. Certain agreements including those between producer and artists or between the channel and the producers etc. are required to be documented.

AGREEMENT FOR AN EXCLUSIVE CONTENT SERVING/ TELECOM RIGHTS IN THE MOBILE SPACE

This Agreement is entered into on __th day of August 2005 BETWEEN _____, a Partnership firm represented by its Partner _____ and having its office at _____, hereinafter referred to as the "**Producers**" (which expression shall unless it be repugnant to the context or meaning thereof mean and include its successors in title, administrators and permitted assigns) of the ONE PART;

AND

_____, a company incorporated under the Companies Act, 1956 and having its registered office at _____ (hereinafter referred to as the "Software Developer" which expression shall unless repugnant to the context or meaning thereof mean and include its respective representatives, administrators and permitted assigns) of the SECOND PART.

WHEREAS:

A. The Producers are engaged in the business of production, distribution and marketing of cinematographic films, including feature films, motion pictures, advertisement films, television serials, music videos etc. and other works within the meaning of the Copyright Act, 1957, for worldwide exploitation on all formats.

B. The Producers own all rights including all intellectual property rights ('IPR') in the film "_____" ("the Film"), starring _____ and others and directed by _____. The Producers also own the rights in each and every component of the Film, which are capable of being commercially exploited separately and distinctly from the Film, for e.g. parts of the Film modified as video clips, wall papers, and screen savers etc., for mobile phones, fixed line devices, other wireless hand held carriers and devices, other telecommunication products and any other products operating in the digital space, commonly known as Content.

C. Software Developer is in the business of developing software applications and Content for mobile phones, fixed line devices and wireless handheld devices and carriers and is recognized as a pioneer in the creation/development/distribution and usage of digital and mobile space for various brands/organizations.

D. The Producers and Software Developer have agreed to enter into an Agreement for the purposes of promoting of the Film whose rights are owned by the Producers by developing the Content which will include but is not limited to graphics (such as wall papers, screen savers, themes, colour logos etc.), mobile games, and video of any format presently available and which may be developed in the future for download on mobile phones, fixed line devices, wireless handheld devices and carriers, other telecommunication devices and any other products operating in the digital space in different geographical markets, including but not limited to India.

E. In pursuance of this objective Software Developer will develop and host the Content of the Film.

NOW THEREFORE IT IS HEREBY AGREED BY AND AMONGST THE PARTIES AS UNDER:

The aforesaid recitals shall form an integral part of this agreement.

1. The Producers hereby grant Software Developer Exclusive Worldwide Telecom Rights for the Film.

   Telecom Rights for the purpose herein means - all rights in connection with and in relation to landline, satellite, wireless telecom instruments and cellular phone handsets, all applications and software programs for such instruments/handsets, including but not limited to true tone, ring back ring tone, themes, screen savers, wall papers, color logos, mobile karaoke, games, SMS, MMS, mobile video clips, video and IVRs that are presently available and any other right that may become available in future. Telecom Rights shall also include rights connected with telecom original equipment manufacturer, and telecom service operators. It shall also include making available full song on telecom instruments.

2. Software Developer will have Exclusive Worldwide Telecom Rights to promote and distribute the Film by enabling the download of the Content through the following distribution channels including but not limited to those mentioned below (hereafter referred as Content Dealers).

   (a) Mobile service providers such as _____, _____.
   (b) Handsets manufacturers such as _____, _____.
   (c) Internet Portals and websites such as _____, _____.
   (d) Content and application providers such as _____, _____.

3. Software Developer shall exclusively develop and market Content, in any of the formats listed below but not limited to or any other derivatives thereof;

   (a) Wallpapers
   (b) Themes
   (c) Operator logos
   (d) Real tones
   (e) True tones
   (f) Games
   (g) Colour logos
   (h) Animated wallpapers
   (i) Caller back tones
   (j) Video
   (k) Voice Promos
   (l) SMS contest
   (m) Mobile applications/programs

However, Software Developer shall not develop any Content from the songs of the Film.

4. Software Developer shall endeavor at all given times to maximize the number of Content Dealers through which the Content can be downloaded. These Content Dealers are not limited to those mentioned in (2) above, but can be any entity operating in the digital space, providing or having the ability to provide Content in digital format to its customers in any part of the world.

5. Software Developer shall decide all arrangement for hosting/making available to consumers the Content for the Film.

6. Where the download of the Content is chargeable to the consumers of the Content Dealers, Software Developer shall enter into agreements with those Content Dealers on terms as it deems fit, to collect royalties, commission, profit shares, monetary compensation of any nature from such Content Dealers.

7. Software Developer shall be entitled to create any further rights/sub-rights/sub-licenses and to obtain sponsorships in respect of the Telecom Rights.

8. Software Developer will pay the Producers the minimum guarantee amount of Rs._____/- ("Guaranteed Amount") as per the following schedule:

Amount	Payment Date
Rs. _____ /- (Rupees _____ only)	On the execution of this Agreement and receipt of materials as described in _____.
Rs._____/- (Rupees _____ only)	On the date of release of the Film.

9a. Software Developer will share 50% of its net revenue generated from the download of the Content through the Content Dealers with the Producers ("Producers Revenue Share"). The Guaranteed Amount of Rs. 1,75,000/- will be treated as an advance against Producers Revenue Share.

9b. It is the responsibility of the Producers to inform Software Developer about the due dates for making payments as per the aforesaid schedule.

9c. Within 15 days after the end of each month _____ Software Developer shall furnish a report to Producers certified by an authorized officer _____ of Software Developer recognizing the amount of net revenue generated in previous month pursuant hereto. Based on such reports, Producers shall quarterly raise an invoice on Software Developer and Software Developer will pay Producers every quarter (within 30 days after receiving the invoice from Producers)

9d. All payments to be made under this Agreement shall be subject to the deduction of tax at source (TDS), wherever applicable, as per provisions of the Income Tax Act, 1961. The aforesaid payment shall be inclusive of all costs, charges, taxes and any other duties levies, as may be applicable.

10. Producers have informed Software Developer that Film will be released by _____, and in case the Film is not released within 3 months of this date, the Producers shall return all monies paid by Software Developer under this agreement with interest @ 18% p.a.

11. Based on the storyline of the Film, and the material provided by the Producers, Software Developer will develop a plethora of Content (at its own cost).

12. The Producers hereby expressly permit Software Developer to develop the Content created around the imagery, audio or using the branding of the Film and allow consumers of the Content Dealers to access it from any network or delivery system deemed fit anywhere in the world.

13. On the execution of the Agreement, the Producers agree to provide Software Developer all images and movie clips and images to create the Content.

14. The Producers agree to promote 'Software Developer' logo and Short Code "_____" in all possible manner, including but not limited to the following:

    (a) "SOFTWARE DEVELOPER" logo and the Short Code ___ shall appear on full screen after appearance of censor certificate but before the actual start of the Film as the exclusive telecom partner along with a call for action eg: "sms (Film name) to _____ (number)" ("Software Developer branding in the Film").

    (b) Insert the Software Developer Logo and the Short Code ___ along with a call for action eg: "sms (Film name) to _____ (number)"" promoting the Content, on all the Film materials such as hoardings, posters, vinyls, on-air promos, TV promotions, trailers, Theatre vinyls, websites, news papers and other co-branded promotion material created for the Film.

    (c) Ensure that wherever, including on all TV Channels, while the movie is promoted, scroll is played displaying the Short Code '___' and 'Software Developer' logo along with a call for action eg: "to _____."

15. The Producers agree to promote Software Developer in marketing & promotional activities of the Film such as Star meets, movie screenings, premier of the film etc. and other PR related activities. The Producers will ensure the presence of leading star cast of the Film i.e. _____ in any marketing & promotional activities including Contests such as "meet & greet stars" organized by Software Developer for promoting the download of the Content. The Producers will also ensure the presence of leading star cast of the Film i.e. _____ for the press conference to be organized by Software Developer to launch the downloadable Content of the Film. Producers shall also provide Software Developer with

costumes of leading starcast of the Film in the Film, which will be used by Software Developer as prizes for the contest to be organized by Software Developer to promote downloadable content of the Film.

16. Producers shall also provide Software Developer with 50 Passes for the Premiere show and 100 tickets per city for the first weekend after release of the Film as prizes for winners of the contest to be organized by Software Developer for promoting the download of the Content.

17. The Producers indemnify and hold Software Developer harmless in consequence or by any of the breach of the representation and warranties (herein) or arising out of any claim alleging that the use of the Content constitutes in any way a breach of any representation and warranties of the Producers (herein) or rights (including intellectual property rights) of any third parties who may have claim over the said Content or the Films. The indemnification shall include any legal cost, punitive or compensatory awards or expenses and disbursements paid by Software Developer on advice of its legal counsel to compromise or settle any claim. The indemnity provisions contained herein shall survive the termination or the expiry of this Agreement.

18. REPRESENTATIONS AND WARRANTIES :

    A. The execution and performance by Software Developer of this Agreement does not conflict with any other agreement entered into by Software Developer.

    B. The license granted by the Producers to Software Developer hereunder is only a limited license for the purposes specified herein and shall not constitute or deem to Software Developer as the owner or a perpetual licensee of the Film or any part thereof.

    C. The execution and performance by Software Developer of this Agreement is within its power and has been duly authorized. It is duly incorporated and validly existing and in good standing.

D. The Producers warrant that the Film or any part thereof, do not contain any material that is obscene, defamatory or licentious.

E. The Producers specifically represent and warrant that they are the exclusive and absolute owners of the Film and they shall grant Software Developer the right to develop and market Content.

F. The Producers specifically represent and warrant that neither they have (except hereunder to Software Developer), nor they will grant Telecom Rights for the Film to any other person whomsoever.

19. Software Developer specifically represents and warrants that it will use the said Content strictly in accordance with the terms as set out in the Agreement.

20. This agreement shall commence from _____ 2006 ("Effective Date") and shall continue unless terminated by the parties in the manner provided herein. Either party shall be entitled to terminate this agreement by giving 30 days written notice to the other party, if other party has committed a material breach of this agreement and the defaulting party does not remedy such breach within 30 days after receipt of notice from other party specifically for the breach.

21. After termination of this Agreement and until all the Content has been removed from the site, which shall not be later than 6 months from the date of such termination or expiry of the Agreement, Software Developer will continue to enable the download of the Content including the download of all such Content which Software Developer has already created/invested in, and Software Developer will share the revenues generated at the agreed percentage (herein) with the Producers till then.

22. All notices, requests and other communications called for by this agreement shall be deemed to have been given immediately if made by telecopy or electronic mail confirmed by concurrent written notice sent to:

If to Producer to:

_____,

_____

And if to the Software Developer to:

_____

_____

Notice by any other means shall be deemed made when actually received by the party to which notice is provided.

23. If any dispute arises amongst parties hereto during the subsistence of this Agreement or thereafter, in connection with the validity, interpretation, implementation or alleged material breach of any provision of this Agreement the parties shall endeavor to settle such dispute amicably. In case of failure by the Parties to resolve the dispute in the manner set out above within 30 days from the date when the dispute arose, the dispute shall be referred to arbitration of a sole arbitrator to be appointed by the parties or in case of disagreement as to the appointment of the sole arbitrator to a panel of arbitrators with each Party nominating one arbitrator and the arbitrators so appointed appointing one arbitrator. The place of the court of arbitration shall be Mumbai. The arbitration proceeding shall be governed by the Arbitration and Conciliation Act, 1996 and shall be in the English language. Each party shall bear their own expenses.

24. The parties agree that they shall, in the performance of this Agreement, comply with all legal and regulatory requirements as may be applicable from time to time.

25. This Agreement shall be governed and construed in accordance with the laws of India.

26. The Courts of Mumbai shall have exclusive jurisdiction in any matter

arising out of or in connection with this Agreement or the arbitration provisions set out above.

IN WITNESS WHEREOF the parties hereto have set and subscribed their respective hands to these presents on the day, month and year first hereinabove written.

Signed and Delivered by)

the within named)

Producer through its Partner)

_____)

Witness:

Signed and Delivered by)

the within named Software)

Developer through _____)

Pursuant to resolution passed)

by the Board of Directors dated _____)

Witness:

AGREEMENT FOR DISTRIBUTION OF A FILM

This Agreement made and executed at Mumbai on this _____.

BETWEEN

ABC Films, having its registered office at _____ (hereinafter referred to as 'ABC Films', which term, unless repugnant to the context and meaning thereof shall include its heirs, executors, administrators and assigns) of the First part.

AND

DEF Ltd., having its registered office at _____ (hereinafter referred to as "DEF", which term, unless repugnant to the context and meaning thereof shall include its heirs, executors, administrators and assigns) of the Other part.

Whereas ABC Films is in the business of distribution/exhibition of films in India.

Whereas DEF is in business, inter alia of production/distribution of movies/ serials and other related activities. DEF is the Producer of the Cinematographic Film "_____", (hereinafter referred to as "The Said Film"), directed by _____, starring _____.

ABC Films has approached DEF with a proposal to represent DEF to distribute the Cinematographic Film "_____", for the territories mentioned in the annexure.

DEF has agreed to appoint ABC Films to represent DEF for the distribution and promotion of the Cinematographic film "_____", for the territories mentioned herein after.

Now these presents witnesseth and it is hereby agreed by and between the parties hereto as follows:

Whereas

1. The Publicity Budget (wall posters) shall be between Rs._____/- and Rs. _____/-.
2. The Artist visit to the theaters, which includes Boarding/Lodging, Bill for Press Conference, Car expenses, shall be borne by the sponsors referred to DEF by ABC Films. DEF shall bear the air tickets expenses only.
3. ABC Films warrants DEF that the expected Run of "The Said Film" shall be 4 – 6 weeks approx. in the entire circuit mentioned in the annexure.

Film & Television Agreements

4. ABC Films has expressly agreed that they shall collect minimum Guarantee/ Advances between Rs._____ to Rs. _____ within this circuit, mentioned in the annexure herein annexed, before one week of the release of the Cinematographic Film.

5. ABC shall appoint agents to protect copyrights of DEF within the territories mentioned in the annexure annexed hereto, with a maximum budget of Rs. _____, on behalf of DEF.

6. Whereas DEF shall have the agreements/understandings with the exhibitors directly within the territory mentioned herein after.

7. It is agreed between the parties that ABC Films shall be paid 10% commission on total billing by DEF after receiving/realization of the monies from the exhibitor, which (the monies), ABC Films warrants that they shall/ will collect the monies from the exhibitors on behalf of DEF.

8. Whereas ABC Films shall not have any rights to appoint any Sub Distributor/Sub Distributors within the entire territory for any work whatsoever.

9. Incase of any kind of nonperformance on the parts of ABC Films, DEF shall have the sole right to terminate this contract.

10. ABC Films shall indemnify and keep indemnifying DEF against all claims, demands, notice, action, proceedings, losses, damages, recoveries, charges and expenses which may be made or brought or commenced against DEF with respect to the said representation and/or any other omissions or commissions by ABC Films.

11. In case of any dispute arising between the parties, shall be first resolved amicably by the parties, failing which the same shall be referred to the sole arbitrator jointly appointed by the parties under the provisions of the Arbitration and Conciliation Act, 1996. Arbitration proceedings shall be conducted at _____ in English language in accordance with the provisions of the Act and/or any amendments hereto. The award of

the arbitration proceedings will be final and binding on both the parties.

12. This Agreement shall be governed by and construed in accordance with the laws of India. Any dispute or difference not being the subject matter of the above-mentioned Arbitration proceedings shall be subject to the jurisdiction of the courts of Law at Calcutta.

For DEF Limited.　　　　　For ABC Films

———————————　　　———————————

Authorised Signatory　　　Authorised Signatory

Television contracts
Agreement for Assignment

This Agreement is entered into on _____ day of _____ BETWEEN _____ having its address at _____, hereinafter referred to as the "Licensor" (which expression shall unless it be repugnant to the context or meaning thereof mean and include its successors and heirs in title, administrators and permitted assigns) of the ONE PART;

AND

_____, a company incorporated under the Companies Act, 1956 and having its registered office at (hereinafter referred to as the "Licencees" which expression shall unless repugnant to the context or meaning thereof mean and include its respective representatives, administrators and permitted assigns) of the SECOND PART.

WHEREAS :

A. The Licensors are engaged in the business of production, distribution and marketing of cinematographic films, including feature films, motion pictures, advertisement films, television serials, music videos etc. and other works within the meaning of the Copyright Act, 1957, for worldwide exploitation on all formats.

B. The Licensors own all rights including all intellectual property rights ('IPR') in the serial as described in Annexure A ("the Serial"). The Licensors also own the rights in each and every component of the Serial - _____, which are capable of being commercially exploited

C. Licensees are engaged in the business of production, distribution and marketing of cinematographic films, including feature films, motion pictures, advertisement films, television serials, music videos etc. and other works within the meaning of the Copyright Act, 1957, for worldwide exploitation on all formats.

D. The Licensor hereby agree to license and the Licensee agree to accept exclusive rights for commercial exploitation in respect of ____ episodes (having duration of ____ mins each) which will be telecasted 1 with1 non prime time repeat within 20 hours, two natural repeats within 1 week on _____ channel for Indian Territory.

E. In pursuance of this objective, the Licensees will host the Content of the Serial _____.

NOW THEREFORE IT IS HEREBY AGREED BY AND AMONGST THE PARTIES AS UNDER:

1. The Licensee hereby agree to take the sole and exclusive License of all the commercial of broadcasting to and for the public of the said Serial to the exclusion of all other persons in the Indian market for _____ channel only and the Licensees hereby agree to accept such License of the said Serial

2. The Licensee shall have the creative liberties to colour correct/edit/repackage/song redubbing of the said Serial without changing the content thereof with the final approval resting with licensor.

3. The Licensee shall make the payment of **royalty** of Rs. _____ only to the Licensor at the time of signing this agreement and against delivery of all the tapes of the ___ episodes of the Serial in ____ format. The Licensee has done technical check and verification of the quality of the tapes at the time of signing of the contract.

4. The Licensee shall have the exclusive rights to promote/advertise/market the said Serial in India for telecast on _____channel only, without any interference from the Licensor or any other person. It will be promoted as _____.

5. The exhibition of the said Serial can be (carried out and completed by the Licensee any time within one year of the signing of the agreement with a grace period of three months after the one year. After the expiry of this period the updated tapes (after colour correction/re dubbing) will be handed over to the Licensor and the Licensee will have no right over the said tapes. The tapes remain the property of licensor at all times.

6. The Licensor shall indemnify the Licensee from any disputes/litigation if

any that may arise for the telecast/advertising of the episodes.

7. The Licensors declare that they have in themselves the exclusive and unencumbered rights in respect of the said Serial worldwide and declare that they have not at any time prior to this agreement transferred/mortgaged or created any third party rights in connection with the said Serial and agree to indemnify the Licensee in case of any claim made by any third party in respect of the said Serial.

8. The Licensee shall have the right to License the rights of commercial exploitation of the said Serial to _____ channel only.

9. The Licensor will at the request of the Licensee assist the Licensee in promotion of the said Serial.

10. At the time of completion of this agreement, the Licensee will have the first right of making an offer within the contracted period, to produce/make a sequel of the serial on mutually agreed terms with the Licensors.

11. If any dispute arises amongst parties hereto during the subsistence of this Agreement or thereafter, in connection with the validity, interpretation, implementation or alleged material breach of any provision of this Agreement the parties shall endeavor to settle such dispute amicably. In case of failure by the Parties to resolve the dispute in the manner set out above within 30 days from the date when the dispute arose, the dispute shall be referred to arbitration of a sole arbitrator to be appointed by the parties or in case of disagreement as to the appointment of the sole arbitrator to a panel of arbitrators with each Party nominating the presiding arbitrator and the arbitrators so appointed appointing one arbitrator. The place of the court of arbitration shall be Delhi. The arbitration proceeding shall be governed by the Arbitration and Conciliation Act, 1996 and shall be in the English language. The arbitrator/arbitral panel shall also decide on the costs of the arbitration proceedings.

12. The Courts of Delhi shall have exclusive jurisdiction in any matter arising out of or in connection with this Agreement or the arbitration provisions set out above.

IN WITNESS WHEREOF the parties hereto have set and subscribed their hands to these presents on the day, month and year first hereinabove written.

Signed and Delivered by	)
the within named	)
Licensor	)
By the hand of its Authorized Signatory	)
	)
Signed and Delivered by	)
the within named	)
	)
By the hand of its Authorized Signatory	)
Mr.	)

Annexture A

T.V. Serial : _____

Hindi Colour

Format: : _____

Produced by:

Directed by:

Total of episodes:

Starring:

Licensed Territory: INDIA Satellite for _____ channel only

Contracted Period : _____

18
Legal Terms

1. *Inter alia* - Among other things.
2. *Ab Initio* - From its inception. For e.g. a contract entered into by 2 persons for sale and purchase of weapons for mass destruction is void *ab initio.*
3. *Suo Motto* - on your own. For e.g. under the Indian Constitution judges can act *suo motto* and treat a letter as a Writ Petition.
4. Estoppel - admission E.g. If a witness in a court proceeding has given a particular version of the facts, he is then estopped (by reason of his own admission) from changing his stance.
5. *Adjournment* - Postponed for another time or place. For e.g. A Judge has the power to adjourn a hearing to another date if the lawyer of the Defendant or the Plaintiff is not well or is indisposed.
6. *Ad-Interim* - For the time being.
7. *Cognizance* - Knowledge or recognition by the Courts of law of facts provided to them.
8. *Animus testandi* - With an intention to make a Will.
9. *Ex-Parte Orders* - Orders issued in the presence of only one or more parties, but in the absence of the other party/ies.
10. *Mens Rea* - Intent to commit an offence.
11. *Quid Pro Quo* - Providing a valuable thing to another in exchange of a

valuable thing from the other.
12. *Culpable* - guilty/chargeable.
13. *Agnate* - Descendent of a common male ancestor.
14. *Sanad* - A document showing ownership to land or office.
15. *Voidable* - Can be avoided/terminated at the option of the party who has been wronged.
16. *Benamidar* - A person who is shown to be the owner of a right mentioned in a Benami transaction, but who in reality is not the owner.
17. *Domicile* - Place where a man permanently resides.
18. *Vakalatnama* - A document executed by a client appointing a lawyer to represent him in a Court of Law. For e.g. A, who wants to file a Suit against B, must first execute a Vakalatnama in favour of a lawyer, who will represent him in the Court.
19. *Addendum* - a thing in addition or that is to be added.
20. *Wakf* - Bequest by a Muslim of his property for any religious, pious or charitable purpose.
21. *Ad-idem* - Agreeing on the same thing in the same sense. If the parties are at a mistake as to the subject matter of the contract entered into by them, the contract is void as the parties are not *ad idem* as to the subject matter.
22. *Bequest* - disposition of property by a person under a Will.
23. *Ad Hoc* - established for a particular purpose.
24. *Vicarious Liability* - Liability imposed on a person for acts committed by another. For e.g. A master is *vicariously liable* for any offence committed by his servant in the course of his duties.
25. *Sub-Judice* - Final Order by the Court is pending.
26. *Carte Blanche* - A piece of paper bearing signatures of one or more persons and leaving space for making a note or any other writing.
27. *Perjury* - giving false testimony
28. *Child en ventre sa mere* - An unborn child.

29. *Bonafide* - in good faith
30. *Witness* - any person acting as evidence of an event.
31. *Amicable* - agreed by all the parties
32. *Audi Alteram Partem* - (a Latin phrase) - No man should be punished without giving him a fair hearing.
33. *Suit* - proceedings instituted in a Court of law for protecting or defending rights
34. *Guardian* - is a custodian of property and person of a minor or any other person who is not capable of managing his own affairs. For e.g. Parents are the natural *guardians* of their (minor) children
35. *Pari Passu* - at the same time.
36. *Res Judicata* - Any legal proceeding for which a final order has been issued
37. *Ejusdem Generis* - of similar kind.
38. *Jurisdiction* - power of a Court or the judge to hear and decide a case.
39. Karta - used in the context of a Hindu Undivided Family (HUF) is the representative of the HUF.
40. Predecessor - one who has preceded another. Example - C purchased a flat from B who had bought it from A. Therefore A is predecessor in title of the flat to B.
41. Amnesty - an act of forgiveness. E.g. Where parties to an Agreement for sale of a flat have not paid the requisite stamp duty at the relevant time, they can do so under the 'Amnesty scheme' of the Government.
42. *Attornment* - Acknowledgement by the Tenant of a new Landlord.
43. Title - is a capacity which a person has in relation to a right or property.
44. Prima facie - on the face of it.
45. ipso facto - by the fact itself.
46. quash - to annul. Example - An appeal filed by Shah Realtors against their suppliers to a higher court (from an order of a lower court) was quashed (set aside) by the higher court.